Communication, Language and Literacy

Other titles in the Supporting Development in the Early Years Foundation Stage series

Also available from Bloomsbury

Communication, Language and Literacy

Nichola Callander and Lindy Nahmad-Williams

Supporting Development in the Early Years Foundation Stage

Bloomsbury Academic
An imprint of Bloomsbury Publishing Plc

B L O O M S B U R Y
LONDON · NEW DELHI · NEW YORK · SYDNEY

Bloomsbury Academic
An imprint of Bloomsbury Publishing Plc

50 Bedford Square	1385 Broadway
London	New York
WC1B 3DP	NY 10018
UK	USA

www.bloomsbury.com

BLOOMSBURY and the Diana logo are trademarks of Bloomsbury Publishing Plc

First published in 2010 by Continuum International Publishing Group Ltd
Reprinted 2012 (twice)
Reprinted by Bloomsbury Academic 2014

Photographs 4.1, 4.2, 6.1 used by kind permission of Paul Hopkins - MMI
educational consultancy services - http://www.mmiweb.org.uk.
Photographs 2.1, 2.2, 3.2, 3.3, 4.3, 5.1, 5.2 and 6.2 used by kind permission of
Emma Jordan E-Services www.emmajordan-eservices.co.uk.
Photographs 1.1, 3.1, 4.1, 5.2, 6.1, 6.3 taken by and used
by kind permission of Lindy Nahmad-Williams.

British Library Cataloguing-in-Publication Data
A catalogue record for this book is available from the British Library.

ISBN: HB: 978-1-4411-0355-0
PB: 978-1-4411-2898-0

Library of Congress Cataloging-in-Publication Data
Callander, Nichola.
Communication, language and literacy/Nichola Callander and
Lindy Nahmad-Williams.
p. cm. – (Supporting development in the early years foundation stage)
Includes bibliographical references and index.
ISBN: 978-1-4411-2898-0 (pbk.)
ISBN: 978-1-4411-0355-0 (hardcover)
1. Children-Language. 2. Oral communication. 3. Reading (Early childhood)
4. Language arts (Early childhood) I. Title. II. Series.
LB1139.L3C34 2010
372.6'049-dc22

2010002887

Series: Supporting Development in the Early Years Foundation Stage

Typeset by Newgen Imaging Systems Pvt Ltd, Chennai, India
Printed and bound in Great Britain

Contents

Author Details

The authors of this book are experienced educationalists with expertise in communication, language and literacy in the early years.

Nichola Callander

Nichola Callander is a Senior Lecturer in Primary and Early Years Education at Edge Hill University. She currently holds the post of Primary and Early Years Core English Co-ordinator working across Primary, Early Years and Key Stage 2/3 programmes. Before taking up her first post at Edge Hill University, she worked for 12 years as a class teacher in an inner city infant school in Lancashire. This context gave her the opportunity to develop a particular interest in the learning of children with English as an additional language. She is currently involved in research with an early career professional, focusing on developing children's attitudes to writing in the early years.

Lindy Nahmad-Williams

Lindy Nahmad-Williams, one of the series editors, is a Senior Lecturer in Primary Education with responsibility for coordinating learning in the early years at Bishop Grosseteste University College Lincoln. Her interests include language development, English and drama and different contexts for learning. She has taught in primary schools in South Yorkshire, Humberside and North Lincolnshire. She has also worked as a Registered Nursery OFSTED inspector and supported teachers in schools across North Lincolnshire in developing language and literacy provision.

Series Editors' Preface

Introduction to the series

Before the 10 year strategy (DfES, 2004) and the Childcare Act of 2006, provision for children under 5 years of age was encompassed in a variety of guidance, support and legislation; *Curriculum Guidance for the Foundation Stage* (QCA, 2000), the *Birth to Three Matters* framework (Surestart, 2003), and the *National Standards for Under 8s Daycare and Childminding* (DfES, 2003). This was confusing for many professionals working with young children. The introduction of Early Years Foundation Stage (DCSF, 2008), brought together the main features of each and has provided a structure for the provision of care and education for children from birth to 5 years of age. More importantly it recognized the good practice that existed in each sector of provision and gives a framework or support for further development.

Learning in the Early Years Foundation Stage

The four themes that embody the principles of the Early Years Foundation Stage (EYFS), (DCSF, 2008) succinctly embody the important features of early years provision.

A Unique Child, identifies the importance of child centred provision, recognizing the rapid development in young children and that each child is capable of significant achievements during these years. It is important not to underestimate young children, who may be capable of action, thinking beyond our expectations. It is easy to think that children are too young or not experienced enough to engage in some ideas or activities, but we need to be open-minded as children are very good at exceeding our expectations. Some children may have particular talents, whilst others may be 'all-rounders'. Some children may have particular needs or disabilities. Each child is unique and it is our challenge to ensure that we meet their particular needs, supporting them and challenging them in their development.

Positive Relationships are essential whilst we support and challenge children so that they move from dependence to independence, familiarity to unfamiliarity, learning how to be secure and confident individuals who begin to understand themselves and others. Positive relationships are key to all areas of children's development. Emotional development requires children to have attachments and positive relationships, initially with close family members, but increasingly with secondary carers, peers and other adults. The link between emotional and social development is very strong and positive relationships will also help children to become independent and develop new relationships and begin to see their position and role in society. Positive relationships also support language development, understandings about the world, a range of skills and indeed play a part in all development.

The context in which children develop play a vital part in supporting them in all areas of development. These contexts need to be **Enabling Environments**, or environments that are secure and make children feel confident, that stimulate and motivate children and which support and extend their development and learning. The environment is made up of the physical and the atmospheric. Both need to be warm and secure, so that children feel safe and comfortable and both need to be motivating to encourage children to explore and learn. The environmental atmosphere is also created by the social interactions of all concerned, providing the security that enables a child to move away from the familiar and explore the unfamiliar in a secure and safe way. Indoor environments should provide opportunities for social interaction, language development and creative activities. Outdoor environments may encourage children to develop physically and an interest in the world around them and with opportunities to explore the familiar and unfamiliar world.

Learning and Development indicates the importance of individual children's unique development and learning. As every child is unique, so they have different learning and development needs and will develop in different ways and at different rates. It is important not to assume that all children develop at the same rate. We know that some children begin to walk or talk at a very early age, whilst others take longer, but this does not indicate what they are capable of achieving later in life. Provision for all children needs to be differentiated. In the early years, this is best done by open-ended activities and differentiated interaction and support. Open-ended activities allow children to use and develop from previous experiences and to differentiate for themselves. Support through modelling, questioning and direction can come from experienced peers and adults and will enable the individual child to develop at a rate appropriate for them.

Working within the Early Years Foundation Stage is not without it challenges. Whilst the principles recognize the individual nature of children and their needs, providing this is a different matter. The Early Years Foundation Stage encompasses children in two traditionally distinct phases of development; from birth to 3 years of age and from 3 to 5 years of age. It involves the integration of three overlapping, but traditionally distinct areas of care; social, health and education. Children will have different needs at different ages and in different areas and stages within the EYFS and the challenge is for professionals to meet these diverse needs. It maybe that the norm for children at each age and stage is quite wide and that as many children fall outside of the norm as within it. Care is needed by professionals to ensure that they do not assume that each child is 'normal'.

In order to effectively support children's development in the Early Years Foundation Stage professionals need to have an understanding of child development and share knowledge and understanding in their area of expertise with others whose expertise may lie elsewhere. Professionals from different areas of children's care and provision should work together and learn from each other. Social care, health, educational professionals can all learn from an integrated approach and provide more effective provision as a result. Even within one discipline, professionals can support each other to provide more effective support. Teachers, teaching assistants, special needs coordinators and speech therapists who work in an integrated way can provide better support for individuals. Paediatricians, paediatric nurses, physiotherapist, opticians etc., can support the health care and physical development of children in a holistic way. Early years professionals, behaviour therapists and child psychologists can support the social and emotional development of children. This notion of partnership or teamwork is an important part of integrated working, so that the different types of professionals who work with young children value and respect each other, share knowledge and understanding and always consider the reason for integration; the individual child, who should be at the heart of all we do. Good integrated working does not value one aspect of development above all others or one age of children more than another. It involves different professionals, from early career to those in leadership roles, balancing the different areas of development (health, social, emotional and educational) and ages, ensuring that the key principles of good early years practice are maintained and developed through appropriate interpretation and implementation of the Early Years Foundation Stage.

Another challenge in the Early Years Foundation Stage is to consider the child's holistic progression from birth, through the EYFS to Key Stage 1 and beyond. Working with children in the Early Years Foundation Stage is like being asked to write the next chapter of a book; in order to do this effectively, you need to read the earlier chapters of the book, get to know the main characters and the peripheral characters, understand the plot and where the story is going. However, all the time you are writing you need to be aware that you will not complete the book and that someone else will write the next chapter. If professionals know about individual children, their families, home lives, health and social needs, they will understand problems, issues, developmental needs and be better placed to support the child. If they know where are child will go next, about the differences between the provision in the EYFS and KS1 and even KS2 (remembering the international definition of early childhood is birth to 8 years of age), they can help the child to overcome the difficulties of transition. Transitions occur in all areas of life and at all ages. When we start new jobs, move house, get married, meet new people, go to university, the transition takes some adjustment and involves considerable social and emotional turmoil, even when things go smoothly. As adults we enter these transitions with some knowledge and with a degree of choice, but young children are not as knowledgeable about the transitions that they experience and have less choice in the decisions made about transitions. Babies will not understand that their mother will return soon, small children will not understand that the friends that they made at playgroup are not attending the same nursery or that the routines they have been used to at home and at playgroup have all changed now that they have gone to nursery or started in the foundation unit at school. Professionals working with children, as they move though the many transitions they experience in the first 5 years, need to smooth the pathway for children to ensure that they have smooth and not difficult transitions.

An example of holistic thematic play

Whilst sitting outside a café by the sea in the north of England, the following play was observed. It involved four children representing the whole of early years from about 2 years of age to about 8 years of age; one was about 2 years of age, another about 3 years of age, one about 5 years of age and the fourth about 7 or 8 years of age. The two older children climbed on top of a large wooden seal sculpture and started to imagine that they were riding on top of a swimming seal in the sea. They were soon joined by the 3-year-old child who sat at the foot of the sculpture. 'Don't sit there' said the eldest, 'You are in the sea, you will drown. Climb on the tail, out of the sea'. The two older children helped the 3 year old to climb onto the tail and she and the 5 year old started to slide down the tail and climb up again. Then the children began to imagine that the cars parked nearby were 'whales' and the dogs out with their owners were 'sharks' and as they slid down the tail they squealed that they should 'mind the sharks, they will eat you'. The 5 year old asked what the people sitting outside the café were and the 8 year old said 'I think they can be fishes swimming in the sea'. 'What about the chairs and tables?' asked the 3 year old, to which the older children replied that, 'they can be fishes too'.

At this point, the 2 year old came up to the children and tried to climb up the seal. The three children welcomed her, helped her climb up onto the tail and join them and asked her what her name was. They continued to play and then the mother of the eldest child came to see if the 2 year old was ok and not being squashed in the sliding down the tail. The children did not welcome the interference of an adult and asked her to go away, because 'we are playing, we are playing'. The mother helped the 2 year old to climb down off the seal and the child started to 'swim' on the floor back towards the seal and the other children. The mother said, 'Oh you are getting dirty, get up', but the child kept on 'swimming'. 'Are you being a dog' said the mother 'don't crawl', but the child shook her head and carried on 'swimming' towards the seal, avoiding the fish and sharks!

In this play episode, the children were engaged in holistic play involving aspects of

- Personal, Social and Emotional Development (cooperation);
- Language, Literacy and Communication (communicating with each other and with adults);
- Knowledge and Understanding of the World (applying ideas about animals that live in the sea);
- Creative Development (imaginative play, involving both ludic or fantasy play and epistemic play, or play involving their knowledge).

The adult intervention was, in this case, unhelpful and did not aid the play and illustrates the importance of adults standing back and watching before they interact or intervene.

Supporting development in the Early Years Foundation Stage

This book series consists of six books, one focusing on each of the key areas of the Early Years Foundation Stage and with each book having a chapter for each of the strands that make up that key area of learning. The chapter authors have between them a wealth of expertise in early years provision, as practitioners, educators, policy-makers and authors and are thus well placed to give a comprehensive overview of the sector.

The series aims to look at each of the key areas of the EYFS and support professionals in meeting challenges of implementation and effectively supporting children in their early development. The aim is to do this by helping readers, whether they are trainee, early career or lead professionals:

- to develop deeper understanding of the Early Years Foundation Stage,
- to develop pedagogical skills and professional reflectiveness,
- to develop their personal and professional practice.

Although the series uses the sub-divisions of the key areas of learning and strands within each key area, the authors strongly believe that all areas of learning and development are equally important and inter-connected and that development and learning for children in the early years and beyond is more effective when it is holistic and cross curricular. Throughout the series, links are made between one key area and another and in the introduction to each book specific cross curricular themes and issues are explored. We recognize that language development is a key element in social and emotional development, as well as development in mathematics and knowledge and understanding of the world. We also recognize that the development of attitudes such as curiosity and social skills are key to development in all areas, recognizing the part that motivation and social construction play in learning. In addition, the books use the concept of creativity in its widest sense in all key areas of development and learning and promote play as a key way in which children learn.

Although we believe it is essential that children's learning be viewed holistically, there is also a need for professionals to have a good knowledge of each area of learning and a clear understanding of the development of concepts within each area. It is hoped that each book will provide the professional with appropriate knowledge about the learning area which will then support teaching and learning. For example, if professionals have an understanding of children's developing understanding of cardinal numbers, ordinal numbers, subitizing and numerosity in problem solving, reasoning and numeracy then they will be better equipped to support children's learning with developmentally appropriate activities. Although many professionals have a good understanding of high quality early years practice, their knowledge of specific areas of learning may vary. We all have areas of the curriculum that we particularly enjoy or feel confident in and equally there are areas where we feel we need more support and guidance. This is why each book has been written by specialists in each area of learning, to provide the reader with appropriate knowledge about the subject area itself and suggestions for activities that will support and promote children's learning.

Within each chapter, there is an introduction to the key area, with consideration of the development of children in that key area from birth to 3 years of age; 3 to 5 years of age; into Key Stage 1 (5 to 7 years of age). In this way we consider the holistic development of children, the impact of that development on the key area and the transition from one stage of learning to another in a progressive and 'bottom-up' way. Chapters also contain research evidence and discussions of and reflections on the implications of that research on practice and provision. Boxed features in each chapter contain practical examples of good practice in the key area, together with discussions and reflective tasks for early career professionals and early years leaders/managers, which are designed to help professionals at different stages in their career to continue to develop their professional expertise.

Jane Johnston and Lindy Nahmad-Williams

Books in the series

Broadhead, P., Johnston, J., Tobbell, C. & Woolley, R. (2010) *Personal, Social and Emotional Development.* London: Bloomsbury

Callander, N. & Nahmad-Williams, L. (2010) *Communication, Language and Literacy.* London: Bloomsbury

Beckley, P., Compton, A., Johnston, J. & Marland, H. (2010) *Problem Solving, Reasoning and Numeracy.* London: Bloomsbury

Cooper, L., Johnston, J., Rotchell, E. & Woolley, R. (2010) *Knowledge and Understanding of the World.* London: Bloomsbury

Cooper, L. & Doherty, J., (2010) *Physical Development*. London: Bloomsbury

Compton, A., Johnston, J., Nahmad-Williams, L. & Taylor, K. (2010) *Creative Development*. London: Bloomsbury

References

DCSF (2008) *The Early Years Foundation Stage; Setting the Standard for Learning, Development and Care for Children from Birth to Five; Practice Guidance*. London: DCSF

DfES (2003) *National Standards for Under 8s Daycare and Childminding*. London: DfES

DfES (2004) *Choice for Parents, the Best Start for Children: A Ten Year Strategy for Children*. London: DfES

QCA (2000) *Curriculum Guidance for the Foundation Stage*. London: DFEE

Surestart, (2003) *Birth to Three Matters*. London: DfES

Introduction to Communication, Language and Literacy

Communication, language and literacy

Communication, language and literacy are the foundations of learning, and they provide essential life skills. Our ability to communicate our thoughts and feelings to others, interact socially and understand the pragmatics of conversations enables us to form relationships and friendships and become successful and confident members of our community. Our ability to read and write gives us access to all other areas of the curriculum, provides us with the means to access texts to read for pleasure and information and allows us to express ourselves in writing and communicate with others through the written word. These essential skills impact on all areas of a child's life, and it is essential that adults understand how to support and promote children's development in speaking, listening, reading and writing.

Sensitive verbal and non-verbal communication with babies and young children encourage positive interactions by which the young child's communication is valued and reciprocated. Sharing books, singing songs, saying rhymes, putting actions to songs and rhymes, joining in play all support language development. This in turn raises children's self-esteem and confidence as they learn that their contributions are recognized, and they appreciate the enjoyment of sharing experiences and communicating with the special people in their lives. This has a direct impact on their personal, social and emotional development (see Broadhead et al., 2010) as the more positive and enjoyable their interactions are the more confident, secure and independent they will become. Children's use of language allows them to develop their thoughts and express their ideas. Children's developing use of vocabulary provides a shared language for key concepts within all other areas of learning. For example, in *Problem Solving, Reasoning and Numeracy* (see Beckley et al., 2010), children learn labels for counting and names of shapes and articulate their thoughts when tackling mathematical problems; in *Knowledge and Understanding of the World* (see Cooper et al., 2010), key scientific vocabulary supports an understanding of new and developing concepts; in *Creative Development* (see Compton et al., 2010), words support imagination and self-expression. All the areas of learning are supported by children's use of language, including questioning, discussing, explaining, expressing ideas, offering opinions and advice, debating and speculating.

It is also vitally important to acknowledge the significance of non-verbal communication. Physical development (see Cooper and Doherty, 2010) enables children to become more aware of their bodies and allows them express themselves physically with increasing self-control. As adults, we need to listen to children's non-verbal expression as well as their verbal expression. This includes facial expressions and body language by which children communicate their feelings and express emotions, which are explored more fully in this series in *Personal, Social and Emotional Development* (Broadhead et al., 2010). Children's creative expression, including their drawings, paintings, making music and dance (see Compton et al., 2010), should also be acknowledged as a valuable means of communication. We must not only see communication, language and literacy as reading and writing, but view them in their broadest sense as the way in which children express themselves culturally, emotionally, socially and intellectually. It is our role to ensure we keep this at the heart of our practice regardless of changes in legislation and new initiatives. As professionals, we need to retain the key principles of good practice and develop our own philosophy based on knowledge of how young children learn and develop. This book aims to support the development of this philosophy by providing an opportunity to reflect on children's learning in communication, language and literacy so that we can evaluate and develop our own practice.

Holistic development in communication, language and literacy

Learning in the Early Years Foundation Stage (EYFS) is not and should not be compartmentalized into separate areas or subjects. Play is central to a child's learning and provides opportunities for development in all different areas of learning.

The reception teacher wanted to encourage more children to use the reading area and tried to make it as attractive as possible. She put floor cushions down, had tape recorders and ear phones for listening to stories and had an author of the month table with books by the same author. On this occasion, the books were by Martin Waddell, and 'Owl Babies' (Waddell, 1992) was the feature book. The teacher had branches of a tree going up the wall and brown material on the floor under the branches to act as a nest. This was under a table which was draped in brown material that could be pulled down to make a den. Torches were supplied to be used in the den. There were several soft toy baby owls in the reading area and some owl glove puppets. There was also a selection of non-fiction books about owls, other birds of prey, night-time and nocturnal animals. There was a writing area just outside the reading area, which was equipped with paper, pencils, crayons, scissors and sticky tape, where children could draw, write and make things out of paper.

The children used the area in different ways during the week. The den was particularly popular with both boys and girls. They would often pretend to be asleep and say goodnight as they pulled down the brown material to make the den, which was dark. They played with the torches, shining them onto things and noting the change in size of the circle of light. They enjoyed shining them through the material and moving them quickly to make the light dart around. Some children played at being owls and mice with the owls jumping out of the den as the mice scuttled past. The puppets were used inside the den, sometimes retelling the story but at other times used in new stories the children made up themselves.

Abby used the writing table to draw all the nocturnal animals she could find in the books and then she wrote what they were underneath. Matthew tried to make filters for the torch with different coloured pieces of paper. He concentrated hard on trying to cut circle the same size as the end of the torch. Lottie lined all the soft toys up and taught them nursery rhymes although she didn't like it when Ashley came to join in and tried to push her away. Ashley persisted and Lottie told her to sit with the owls, which she did with her legs crossed. Lottie told her she was 'sitting up very smartly' and the play continued with Lottie in the role of teacher and Ashley in the role of a child in Lottie's class. Jason and Emma looked through the book on birds of prey together and Jason talked about seeing a sparrow hawk 'hovering' in the sky. Katie liked to listen to the stories on the tape. All of the children knew the author Martin Waddell and the story of 'Owl Babies' (Waddell, 1992).

Although the area had a literacy focus, all other areas of learning were explored. Within communication, language and literacy, children were talking together, listening, discussing, making up stories, sharing books, reading and writing and could use elements of book talk. They were also learning about a children's author. Other areas of the EYFS (DCSF, 2008) included

- Personal, social and emotional development, by taking on roles and applying the social rules, managing conflict and negotiating to solve problems, perseverance and independence (see Broadhead et al., 2010);
- Problem solving, reasoning and numeracy, by an awareness of shape and space when using the torches and trying to make filters to fit (Beckley et al., 2010);
- Knowledge and understanding of the world, by finding out about birds and other animals, light and dark, and day and night, exploring light and transparency and making filters (Cooper et al., 2010);
- Creative development, by using their imagination in their role play, building on their previous knowledge and using it in imaginative contexts, singing and using puppets in dramatic play (see Compton et al., 2010) and
- Physical development, by using the den, negotiating space, crawling as mice, drawing, writing and cutting.

Structure of this book

In Chapter 1, 'Language for Communication', Lindy Nahmad-Williams outlines the remarkable way by which children acquire language. There is also a focus on non-verbal communication and the shared meanings within any one culture. Lindy highlights the importance of stories, rhymes and songs and how to create an ethos that values listening and talking. In Chapter 2, 'Language for Thinking', Lindy discusses the way language supports children's understanding of new concepts and how language helps children to make meaning from new and revisited experiences. The importance of narrative is explored with a consideration of how it helps children to make connections and shape their understanding of the world. Chapter 3, 'Linking Sounds and Letters', discusses how children move from verbal language to being able to decode written language. The phonics debate is explored and current initiatives, including the teaching of synthetic phonics, are considered within the context of an appropriate learning environment for young children. In Chapter 4, 'Reading', Nichola Callandar discusses the way in which reading provides richly rewarding experiences that can help children to connect with their culture and with people around them in new and different ways. Consideration is given to the way in which we can encourage young children to engage with and respond to texts. In Chapter 5, 'Writing', Nichola discusses oral language experiences and the writing process and the importance of supporting children through a play-based curriculum. Narrative is discussed through the storying behaviour demonstrated by children through play and how this can then lead to writing. In Chapter 6, 'Handwriting', Nichola discusses the fact that although handwriting may be viewed as a largely physical skill, mastery of this skill enables children to communicate successfully as a writer. The role of the adult in supporting the development of handwriting is explored within a holistic approach to the early years curriculum.

The case studies and reflective tasks will also help professionals to reflect on their own practice, consider the theories and research underpinning effective practice and enable them to identify how they can (and why they should) develop their practice. These case studies are designed at two levels: the early career professional and the early years leader. The early years professionals may be students/trainees who are developing their expertise in working with young children, and for them, the reflective tasks encourage them to look at the case studies and engage in some critical thinking on issues that are pertinent for early years education. They will also be able to use the chapters to develop their understanding of issues in knowledge and understanding of the world and try out some of the ideas to develop their skills supporting children in this important area of development. The reflective tasks for early career professionals are also relevant to professionals who are in the early part of their career and to help them in their day-to-day interactions with children and also to help them to engage in the national debates about good practice and educational theories. The second level of reflective tasks is geared towards the early years leaders, who have a strategic role to develop the practice of those who work with them and also the children in the early years setting. They would be interested on the impact on both the adult professional development but raising standards in knowledge and understanding of the world in young children in their setting. The reflective tasks may well be ones that can be addressed as part of a staff meeting or staff development session and can follow the practical tasks so that professionals at all levels can share ideas and experiences and identify factors affecting their support for children, both positive factors and challenges to overcome. In this way, professionals can discuss their own and others' practice, share successes, support each other and come to realize that there is not one model of good practice, one recipe, that if we all follow will automatically lead to success in children's development and help the setting achieve outstanding recognition in inspections.

We hope that professionals reading this book will enjoy and find the content useful in their professional lives.

References

Beckley, P., Compton, A., Johnston, J. and Marland, H. (2010) *Problem Solving, Reasoning and Numeracy.* London: Continuum

Broadhead, P., Johnston, J., Tobbell, C. and Woolley, R. (2010) *Personal, Social and Emotional Development.* London: Continuum

Compton, A., Johnston, J., Nahmad-Williams, L. and Taylor, K. (2010) *Creative Development.* London: Continuum

Cooper, L. and Doherty, J. (2010) *Physical Development.* London: Continuum

Cooper, L., Johnston, J., Rotchell, E. and Woolley, R. (2010) *Knowledge and Understanding of the World.* London: Continuum

DCSF (2008) *Setting the Standards for Learning, Development and Care for Children from Birth to Five; Practice Guidance for the Early Years Foundation Stage.* London: DCSF

Waddell, M. (1992) *Owl Babies.* London: Walker Books

Language for Communication

Introduction

What is communication?

Communication is the way we convey meaning to each other and, in its broadest sense, is not only a human phenomenon. In the Spring, when I was watching birds with their fledglings in the garden, the fledglings called regularly to their parents for food, opening their beaks and flapping their small wings. Anyone who has had a pet will recognize familiar ways that pets communicate, often going beyond indicating a need for food but also communicating affection and even a sensitive awareness of mood. When discussing communication between humans, however, the most important aspect is the development of relationships and social interactions (DCSF, 2008). Warm and loving relationships are the first step towards a child developing as a skilful communicator, including developing their skills in listening, responding, empathizing and sharing emotions (David et al., 2003).

Communication is fundamental to any society, from the intimacy of one-to-one interaction to the endless possibilities of global communication through a range of technological advances. It is through successful communication that children learn to become members of their community, which includes their family, nursery, school and the wider society in which they live. Humans have an intrinsic need to interact with others, which Bruner (1983) highlighted when stressing the importance of the social and cultural setting in the development of children's communication and language skills. Lindon (2005: 145) highlights the importance of the influence of the 'communication behaviour' of the adults closest to the child. These early interactions provide the foundation for the development of social relationships, friendships and the ability to communicate effectively within society. If this communication behaviour is positive and acts as a good role model, then this should impact effectively on the child's developing communication skills.

People can communicate in a variety of ways, such as through art, music, dance and drama. Bruce (2005) emphasizes the importance of adults sharing music, dance, rhyme and rhythm with children to nurture feelings of involvement and a sense of connection. The Reggio Emelia approach (Edwards et al., 1998), founded by Loris Malaguzzi in Italy just after the Second World War, focuses on the many different ways children can communicate through creative exploration and collaboration which is often referred to as the Hundred Languages of Children. It is important for adults working with young children to recognize the significance of providing opportunities for children to communicate through a range of mediums and experiences.

What is language?

Graddol et al. (1994) debate the many definitions of language as proposed by linguists and language scholars, which shows the complexity of the subject. To put simply, language could be described as a systematic use of symbols to enable us to communicate meaning to one another. As humans, we are the only species that have speech, but it is important to remember that language includes far more than speech. Facial expressions, body language, gestures and vocalizations all contribute significantly to communication. Non-verbal communication has a significant part to play in our interactions with others and is often cited as more important than the spoken word. We are very sensitive to non-verbal signals. Someone's posture and facial expression can immediately signal to us an indication of emotion, such as happiness or anger. If we hear voices coming from another room, we may not hear the words but can tell from the tones and volumes of the voices if there is an argument or if the people are enjoying themselves. Children convey meaning non-verbally, and it is important that adults working with children are sensitive and 'listen' and respond to the signals being conveyed. It is also important to note that children 'read' adults' non-verbal behaviour and this can have a profound effect on their self-esteem and confidence.

Practical task 1.1

Spend 10 minutes observing a colleague working with children and note down all the examples of non-verbal communication evident. Include facial expressions, gesture, posture, eye contact, physical levels and physical distance between adult and children. Try to estimate the percentage of non-verbal communication during the 10 minutes in contrast to the percentage of verbal exchange. Remember to include the non-verbal communication that occurs *with* the verbal communication.

Reflection for early career professional

- How powerful was the non-verbal communication? In what way?
- How could you tell that there was a response to the non-verbal communication?
- What have you learnt about non-verbal communication from this observation?

Reflection for leader/manager

- How do your staff differ in their use of non-verbal communication?
- What are the examples of good practice that you would like to promote?
- How do you include children's non-verbal communication in assessments?
- What can you learn about children from these assessments, both planned and incidental?

Language acquisition is an area that has a number of different and conflicting theoretical explanations. The behaviourist theory (Skinner, 1953) emphasizes the role of the child imitating speech and this being reinforced by the adults, whereas the nativist approach (Chomsky, 1972) disagrees with this and asserts that we are biologically programmed to learn language and have a Language Acquisition Device (LAD) which allows us to process language. The socio-interactionist approach (Bruner, 1983) emphasizes our intrinsic need to be sociable and requires a Language Acquisition Support System (LASS) in which adults promote and support the development of language. Tomasello (2003) believes in the 'usage-based' theory in which children learn to master language through regular use and cognitive processing. Gasser (2006) believes that there is regularity in language that humans can process through statistical learning mechanisms. The debate is likely to continue, but what is apparent is that children do acquire language remarkably quickly and adults need to be aware of the significance of their role in promoting language development.

The development of speech

Babies experiment with sounds, starting with cooing at about 1 month of age and then at about 4–5 months of age they experiment with speech-like sounds, pitch, blowing bubbles and making noises with the lips. This vocal play (Crystal, 1995) develops into babbling by about 6 months when the baby uses and repeats sounds of speech, particularly consonant and vowel sounds such as 'dadada' (Mukherji and O'Dea, 2000). At this stage, the sounds represent any sound the mouth can make and are not restricted to sounds made in any one particular language. As deaf babies babble, it can be assumed that the babies are not necessarily imitating sounds they hear, but are just experimenting (Herman, 2002). At about 9 months, deaf babies' babbling ceases and hearing babies begin to use sounds that are only present in the language that they are hearing. This can be seen as the first stage of the development of speech.

The first word a baby uses is often seen as a milestone in a child's life. This usually occurs at about 12 months, but for some babies this comes earlier and for others later. From this point on speech development follows a familiar sequence of stages:

1 9–18 months: one-word stage/holophrase, for example mama, doggie, teddy. At 18 months, a child would have learnt about 50 words and from then on would learn one or two new words a day (O'Grady, 2005).
2 18–24 months: two-word stage/pivot grammar – usually nouns plus another word to give a context, for example, daddy gone (daddy has gone to the shops).

3 24–30 months: telegraphic speech – multi-word utterances that lack function words, for example, me daddy car (I want to go in daddy's car).

4 30+ months: children are applying grammatical structures such as plurals and tense endings, even if this results in over-generalizing such as 'He runned'. Children make rapid progress and begin to use more complex sentences.

5 4 or 5 years: by this age, children are using adult-like structures and have a wide vocabulary. Unfamiliar adults should be able to understand what the child is saying.

Children's receptive language (their ability to listen and respond) develops at a faster rate than their expressive (spoken) language. This means that they will understand more words than they can actually say. Tone of voice and facial expressions aid children's understanding of the words being said to them, for example, they soon understand the word 'no' as a negative in comparison to the lighter, more sing-song tone usually used when praising or soothing. Adults usually support each stage of development by extending children's utterances as a model for the standard, grammatical composition of speech. For example, a young child saying 'allgone' may get an adult response such as 'Yes. You've finished your drink; it's all gone' or 'Has it all gone? Would you like some more?' or 'Clever girl – you've drunk it all up'. They may also repeat 'allgone' as positive reinforcement in the very early stages. It is therefore the adult's role to interpret the utterance and respond appropriately to help support children's language development.

Supporting the development of language for communication

For children to form effective relationships and participate fully in society (DCSF, 2008), they must learn pragmatic skills (Bowen, 1998). These include the social skills of language use, including turn taking, conversational skills, appropriate responses and understanding that different contexts may require different language use, such as formal and informal situations. The basis of language for communication is the mastery of these pragmatic skills, and a child's early language experiences will provide the foundations for their development.

There has been recent concern about the rising number of children who have limited language skills on starting school (Linden, 2005). Research conducted by the National Literacy Trust (2005) suggests that there is very little evidence to indicate that this is the case and that it is more about the perception of adults working in early years settings than actual fact. Some of the reasons stated for the decline in language skills are television, computer games and lack of parental time and communication. There are also arguments that suggest that television can promote imaginative play (Marsh, 2005) and that well-managed viewing can be the catalyst for discussion between parent and child. The National Literacy Trust's findings state that the time parents spend with their children has risen steadily since the 1960s rather than being in decline, despite more parents going out to work. Linden (2005:160) suggests we should not blame parents and television as limited language skills on starting school might be due to 'misguided early years practice', while the National Literacy Trust suggests it might be due to early years practitioners' increasing awareness of the importance of language development. I am sure the debate will continue with strong opinions on all sides, but that last point is fundamental. Early years practitioners should not only be aware of the significance of the development of communication, but should also know how to provide a supportive and enabling environment and be aware of sensitive interventions for children who are experiencing difficulties. This chapter will consider a variety of ways to develop an enabling environment for communication and consider how children's difficulties can be supported.

Language for communication from birth to 3 years of age

Communication is the key to forming secure and loving relationships. There is evidence to suggest that a foetus can recognize the pitch and rhythm of its mother's voice when it is still in the womb (David et al., 2003; Kisilevsky et al., 2003). Once born, the touching, looking, smiling, talking and holding that a baby receives establishes a secure bond. This non-verbal communication is a key part of the relationship building. Babies soon learn to recognize their main carers and show a preference for familiar faces and voices. They also communicate non-verbally through gaze, vigorous sucking, touching and grasping (David et al., 2003). When adults communicate with babies, they often use what Linden (2005) terms infant-directed speech, which is also known as motherese. This is often a higher-pitched, more exaggerated and softer voice than that used adult to adult. There is also a tendency to repeat sounds that babies make and imitate their expressions. Bruce and Spratt (2008) discuss the importance of this imitation to the development of communication and the way babies also imitate adults' movements and respond to their expressions.

Songs and rhymes

Trevarthen (2008) has conducted extensive research into the importance of rhythm and movement to companionship and the development of relationships and communication skills. He refers to the pre-verbal interactions between adult and baby as protoconversations, with the way the tones, rhythms and melodies of these conversations help the baby to develop speech. Simple rhymes and songs such as 'Round and Round the Garden', 'This Little Piggie', and 'Incey Wincey Spider', that also incorporate actions and body contact, all help to provide a musical companionship that is present in all societies. We must not underestimate the power of music, rhythm and rhyme as a crucial form of communication, which will continue throughout our lives. Songs and poetry evoke memories and emotions, and most of us can name pieces of music that have special meaning to us, whether it be from childhood, adolescence or 'our' song that has significance in a relationship.

Photograph 1.1 Children listening to rhymes and stories (Photograph by L Nahmad-Williams)

Case study 1

Carol is singing a song to her 5-month-old baby, Amy. As she sings she looks into Amy's eyes and Amy gazes back at her. Carol's voice is very soft and she smiles as she sings. Amy makes cooing, gurgling sounds and smiles. She also begins to move her arms up and down as though dancing or conducting the music. Carol takes one of Amy's hands and they both move their arms up and down as Carol continues to sing. Amy now starts to make higher-pitched squealing and vocalizes more regularly. She moves her head around and grasps her free hand towards her mother.

Amy is now 12 months old. Carol is sitting opposite her daughter on the rug. Amy is sitting up and Carol is singing 'The Wheels on the Bus Go Round and Round' enthusiastically with accompanying actions. Amy jigs her body to the rhythm and waves her arms but stays quiet. At the end of the verse, Amy laughs and leans forward to lift her mother's arms indicating she would like her to sing again. As Carol sings the song a second time, Amy's body moves more vigorously to the rhythm and she flaps her hands during the time her mother rolls her arms to indicate the wheels going round. She also bangs her hands on the floor to the rhythm and again laughs at the end, makes singing noises and leans forward to grab her mother's hands to start again.

Reflection for early career professional

- In what ways is Amy communicating with her mother? How has this developed in the second observation?
- What else could Carol do to involve Amy when singing to her?

Reflection for leader/manager

- How and when does your setting use music, rhythm and rhyme with the children?
- What do you think is the difference between sharing songs on a one-to-one basis and sharing them as a group? How do you ensure there are opportunities for both?

Gestures

It is not only the rhythm of the voice that is important but also the rhythm of the body and movement. Gestures are an important part of communication and babies will often copy the gestures of adults. Goodwin et al. (2000), following their research into babies' use of gesture and infants' use of mime in play, have developed the use of gesture further to a recognized set of symbols to be used as sign language between adults and babies. Baby signing has its critics (Grove et al., 2004), but there are many people who believe the use of signing enhances communication between adult and baby. We must also remember that we use many specific gestures to indicate meaning that babies and young children 'read', such as fingers on lips for quiet, waving for hello or goodbye, thumbs up for well done, shrugging shoulders for 'don't know', shaking our head for 'no' and nodding for 'yes'. In many ways baby signing could just be seen as an extension of the many socially acknowledged signs we already use in our culture.

Sharing books

Sharing books with babies is another way of developing companionship and communication skills. This is something that is nationally recognized, with local authorities running schemes such as 'Books for Babies', which ensure all babies receive a book bag, one or two books and a library card to encourage parents and carers to read to their babies. Evidence from Wade and Moore (1998) suggests that sharing books with babies results in children starting school with more advanced literacy and numeracy skills. I think more important than this is the additional evidence that children also have more developed social skills. This is due to the aspect of sharing, communicating and the developing conversations that occur when reading with babies and young children. This helps to develop the pragmatic skills of turn taking, listening and responding that are so essential to the development of positive relationships.

Language for communication from 3 to 5 years of age

Children aged between 3 and 5 are usually very competent communicators. They have a good mastery of spoken language and have learnt how to use their communication skills to their advantage through use of facial expressions, body language and tone of voice. Children love to experiment with words and sounds, often enjoying nonsense rhymes and putting sound effects to events in stories, such as the roar of a lion, the ring of a bell or the whooshing of the wind. Songs that encourage different sounds, such as 'Old Macdonald had a Farm' or 'I am the Music Man' allow children to experiment and play with the sounds their voices can make. Actions that accompany songs and finger rhymes not only help to develop physical skills but also promote a sense of community through shared actions. Some songs miss out words as the song progresses, as can be done in 'Heads, Shoulders, Knees and Toes', where the action takes the place of each word each time it is repeated. The communication through eye contact, sharing of the coordination and understanding each other's mistakes provides a sense of community and shared experience.

Established routines

Established routines, such as snack time, provide good opportunities for the development of communication skills, including social etiquette. The promotion of good manners, such as 'please' and 'thank you' and the opportunity to speak and listen to one another are a key part of this routine. Research has indicated that mealtimes are when the richest language is used in the home (Fiese and Schwartz, 2008). Snack times can be utilized in a similar way. When I was teaching I used to put on a piece of music while the children were going to the toilet and getting their snack. When we were all seated and eating, we would then discuss the piece of music that had been playing. I remember an Ofsted inspector describing himself as 'speechless' after observing a snack time in my classroom where three 4-year-old boys were discussing the merits of Saint Sans and Vivaldi. If I visit classrooms or nurseries where children are eating their fruit in silence or listening to the teacher talking, I feel that a valuable opportunity for conversation is being lost. Although I see the value in children helping themselves to their fruit as and when they feel like it through the morning, as occurs in some settings, I also see real value in using a routine such as snack time as an equivalent in the setting for mealtimes in the home.

Practical task 1.2

Reflection for early career professional

- How do you organize snack times?
- What opportunities do you provide for children to develop social skills?
- Could you organize snack times differently to promote talk and communication?

Reflection for leader/manager

- Consider how the different classroom routines in your setting develop different social skills. Could any be improved and, if so, how?
- What different stimuli could be used in your setting to promote conversations between children?
- When would these be used and how would they be managed?
- How do you ensure staff/colleagues know their role in these conversations?

Hidden curriculum

The hidden curriculum is an ideal opportunity to show how a setting values communication. The respect that adults show to one another and to the children provides essential role models. The way the setting communicates in writing can be quite significant, for example, are the rules expressed in positive or negative language? An example of positive language would be 'Please close the gate', whereas negative language would be 'Do not leave the gate open'; one focuses on desired behaviour, whereas the other focuses on what not to do. The former promotes a more positive ethos and a more open approach to communication. If children are constantly praised for 'being quiet' and 'not talking' rather than being praised for 'listening' or 'waiting their turn', it could give the message that their talk and participation in conversations are not valued. It is therefore essential that practitioners think carefully about the words they use and the potential messages they are communicating through the hidden curriculum to promote children's language for communication.

Case study 2

The nursery takes children aged 3–5 and is adjacent to a Children's Centre in a deprived, urban area. As the children enter the nursery in the morning the head of the nursery stands at the door and greets each child by name as they enter. The parents and carers come into the nursery with their children and the children know where to hang their coats and collect their name card to put on the daily register. The nursery nurse and teacher have resources set up in the carpet area and the children go straight to the carpet to explore the resources. These include torches, different fabrics, coloured cellophane and kaleidoscopes. Some parents and carers leave straight away; others come up and speak to either the nursery nurse or the teacher about a variety of different things, from a brief message about who will be collecting the child to longer conversations relating to the birth of a new baby and illness of a spouse. None of the parents or carers joins his or her children or talks to them about the resources. The teacher then sits down on the carpet with the children and talks to individuals about the resources and shines a torch through some material. One child shines the torch into another eyes and the teacher immediately says 'point your torch to the ceiling and see what happens?' The child does this and talks excitedly about the light on the ceiling. The parents and carers leave once the teacher joins the children on the carpet. There is no teacher input as she just joins in with the children's explorations.

Reflection for early career professional

- What examples of communication can you identify?
- Consider the non-verbal communication. What signals are used to communicate what children should do as they arrive and what is expected of parents/carers?

Reflection for leader/manager

- What would you say are the key messages that the setting is conveying to the parents/carers and children from the evidence in this short case study? How are these messages communicated? Are there any that you think should be changed and, if so, why?
- Consider the start of sessions in your setting and compare with the case study. What messages do you think your setting communicates to parents/carers and children? Are there any ways that these could be improved?

Puppets

The use of puppets is an excellent way of engaging children in dialogue and stimulating their imagination. They promote communication skills and enrich language use in a non-threatening, playful way. There is a wide variety of puppets available, from the more expensive large, child-like puppets to cheaper versions which are usually smaller and are often animals or imaginary creatures. Children's response to puppets is invariably positive and a source of fun and amusement. Because of this they tend to interact with the puppet freely and enthusiastically.

Puppets can be used by the adult or the children in a number of different ways. It is often practitioners who have to rid themselves of inhibitions to use the puppet that is the most difficult obstacle to overcome. Bentley (2005) suggests there are three ways of using puppets depending on the confidence of the practitioner. The first and the easiest way is to have a silent puppet who watches and responds through movement, but whose actions/feelings are

Photograph 1.2 Puppets

interpreted by the practitioner or children. The second way is to have a puppet who whispers into the ear of the practitioner and the practitioner then appears to be having a dialogue and shares this with the children to enable them to interact. The third and final way is to have a talking puppet that involves the practitioner giving the puppet a voice. There is no need to be a ventriloquist for this approach as the children will fully immerse themselves in the puppet's world. Once this has been achieved, puppets can be used to tell stories, pose problems such as how to make friends or deal with anger, promote manners and social skills, explore feelings and enable children to come to terms with key events in their life such as a new baby in the family or being poorly. The puppet acts as a catalyst and then supports a whole range of communication skills.

Circle time

Circle time is an ideal way of promoting speaking and listening skills in a secure environment. The skills of listening, turn taking, keeping to the subject, responding appropriately and understanding of role are all promoted through circle time. I am slightly concerned about the way circle time has almost become a sacred activity with rules and regulations and a very serious tone. Although it is important there are shared rules, circle time can, and should, be fun too. In many ways, circle time promotes listening more than talking as the children are encouraged to listen to each child in the circle and only speak when it is their turn. The balance is therefore much more towards listening. Of course, this is dependant on the number of children in the circle. It does not have to be the whole class; experimenting with different group sizes can create different opportunities. Activities can also include no speaking at all such as 'pass the squeeze', where children squeeze the hand of the person next to them once their hand has been squeezed. This type of activity promotes sensitivity to one another, response to others and a feeling of being a part of a community. Where the activity does include speaking, it does not particularly promote conversational skills as there is not the natural ebb and flow of listening and responding, but it does give each child the opportunity to voice an opinion, feeling or idea.

Practical task 1.3

List all of the circle time activities that you know. Consider the skills that each one promotes. Can you categorize them so that you are clear about the skills being developed? For example,

- listening
- responding
- remembering
- giving an opinion
- Problem solving
- imagining
- expressing an emotion

Reflection for early career professional

- Try to develop your own circle time activities to develop a range of communication skills.
- Which skills are the easiest to think of ideas for and which are the most difficult?

Reflection for leader/manager

- Consider planning a staff development session on the use of circle time to develop different skills.
- Audit current practice and consider how this could be developed.

Listening to children

As adults we should think of ourselves as partners in conversations with children and this includes genuinely listening to them (Lancaster, 2003). Many practitioners fall into the trap of asking questions for which they already know the answer to check understanding or memory rather than asking a question because they want to know what a child thinks or feels (Alexander, 2004) and respond appropriately. Another trap is asking for a child's opinion but then doing what you intended all along. We all know how it feels when our opinions or ideas do not appear to be valued and it is no different for children. We often make decisions about the classroom organization based on our own perceptions of what would be best for the children rather than asking them. The next time you want to move the classroom furniture around, ask the children how they would like it organized; arrange it together and then it will be a joint venture to the benefit of everyone in the classroom. Of course there may be some suggestions that are not possible due to space or other restrictions, in which case make that clear to the children. Explain why something can't be done rather than just dismissing it.

Case study 3

A primary school asked a professional playworker to come and advise the staff on how to develop the playground and field so that they would be more interesting and promote more opportunities for different types of play. He suggested they included two children from each class onto the committee to discuss ideas and make decisions. This ensured that the playground was being developed for children and by children. He constantly reminded staff of the need to listen to the children's ideas and opinions. One child suggested a fairground ride and it was explained that it would be much too expensive and would need someone to operate it. The child was quite happy with this response. The playworker suggested bark shavings to provide a safe, soft surface under the climbing area. The children were unanimously against this because bark shavings always went into their shoes. The playworker persisted until a member of staff reminded him that we must listen to the children. At this point it was agreed that other surfaces would be investigated and priced.

Reflection for early career professional

- Why do you think the playworker was reluctant to listen to the children on that one point?
- How would you ensure children felt they were being listened to even if their ideas could not be accepted?

Reflection for leader/manager

- Consider whether you have provided any opportunities, such as in the case study, where the setting has made changes based on children's ideas. If so,

⇨

were these successful and why? If not, can you think of an example where this could have been done?

- How could you incorporate this ethos of listening to children into your setting?
- Consider what the benefits would be to both the children and the setting.

Transition to Key Stage 1 (5 to 7 years of age)

Children are now very competent language users and it is important for the practitioner to continue to provide opportunities to develop communication skills. In the EYFS, the children would have been used to sustained periods of play and freedom in their interactions. It is hoped that there would still be many child-initiated play opportunities in Key Stage 1 (KS1) and planned activities to promote speaking and listening skills.

Group discussion and interaction

Speaking and Listening forms one part of the National Curriculum for KS1 (DfEE, 1999), and this includes group discussion and interaction. The next chapter on Language for Thinking will explore this in more depth, but being able to work effectively with others requires good communication skills. Providing children with opportunities to work in groups is possible in all areas of the curriculum. These could include developing a group dance in PE, carrying out a group investigation in science or maths, working on a collaborative story, programming a controllable toy and following instructions together, creating a group collage or painting and designing and making a moveable toy; the possibilities are endless. To guarantee successful group working, children need to have developed good pragmatic skills. They need to understand their role in the group and how to interact with others to the advantage of the whole group. These are skills which need to be taught, particularly if a child's pragmatic skills are not well developed.

There are a variety of different ways practitioners can support this development. Children need to be made aware of the skills they will be developing, and therefore practitioners need to explain to the children the characteristics of effective group work, such as listening to others, trying out each other's ideas, reaching a consensus and suggesting different roles such as chairperson, scribe, spokesperson, etc. Practitioners also need to assess these skills and involve children in self- and peer-assessment. Again this will reinforce the types of skills children are developing and raise the status of these skills. It is also useful to consider the size and formation of the groups depending on the activity. It is important to be aware of group dynamics, which could be affected by ability grouping, friendship grouping, random grouping, size of group and personalities within the group. When reflecting on the success of a group activity, don't only consider whether the task was suitable; also take account of the grouping and children's developing skills to work effectively as a member of a group.

Practical task 1.4

Look at your medium-term planning. Highlight any opportunities for learning in groups. Plan for these in more detail considering the number in a group, the composition of the group, the speaking and listening skills being promoted alongside the main subject objective for the lesson, the way you will assess these skills, organizational issues and outcome of the group activity.

Reflection for early career professional

- Do you include speaking and listening objectives when you plan for learning? If not, consider how to do this on your current medium-term plan. If you do, how do you assess these objectives have been met?

Reflection for leader/manager

- How do you ensure your staff plan explicitly for speaking and listening?
- Ask staff to share the different ways they use group work and consider how this could be developed across the whole setting to promote speaking and listening skills.

Dialogic teaching and learning

Alexander (2004) has written extensively on the importance of a dialogic approach to teaching. At the heart of this approach is the importance of child talk over and above that of teacher talk. He emphasizes the need to listen to children's answers and opinions so that there is not one rule for adults and one rule for children. He states that dialogic teaching is 'collective, reciprocal, supportive, cumulative and purposeful' (2004: 22). This means that the teacher and pupils share conversations equally, build on each others' ideas and thoughts and have a clear purpose to promote learning. This does not mean that the teacher is passive; in fact, it is the exact opposite. It takes a skilled teacher to ensure the talk is purposeful without over-direction, and children feel safe to express their views and be challenged by teachers who in turn accept being challenged by children's responses. Alexander (2004) suggests that dialogic teaching develops a number of key skills, including listening attentively, responding appropriately, framing and asking questions, justifying viewpoints, evaluating ideas and reaching compromises. This approach, which embodies both the key themes of enabling environments and positive relationships, also clearly promotes the pragmatic skills children need to develop effective relationships.

Technology

When discussing communication, it is impossible not to include technology and Information and Communication Technology (ICT). As children get older, much of their communication will be through devices such as mobile phones and computers. This is an ever-changing environment, and whatever I may refer to in this chapter would surely have been replaced by something new and improved by the time the book is published. For this reason, I will not discuss specific examples, but it is necessary for practitioners to be aware of the modes of communication used by children, their family and friends. We need to ensure children are prepared for the twenty-first century, and embracing new technologies with knowledge and discernment should enable practitioners to support children with this aspect of communication.

Working with other professionals

Although many children will develop communication skills without too many difficulties, there are some children who will require additional support. This may be done by staff within the setting, such as supporting children who lack confidence or being a role model for those who have limited language experiences in the home to develop pragmatic skills. There may come a point, however, when other professionals need to be contacted to provide specialized help. This may be related to children for whom English is not their first language or it could be related to children who have delayed communication and language development. Communication difficulties can be due to a number of different aspects. Articulation difficulties can involve problems with certain speech sounds that cannot be pronounced properly and stammering. Language difficulties involve problems with ordering and sequencing thoughts for communication, which also includes difficulties processing the spoken word so that the message received is understood. Therefore, language difficulties can involve both expressive and receptive language. There are many different types of speech and language difficulty, including verbal dyspraxia, autism, selective mutism, Asperger's syndrome and other contributing factors to language delay (for more information on specific needs, see the Afasic website http://www.afasic.org.uk/pub.htm).

It is important that practitioners are aware of the stages of language development so that they can identify potential difficulties. It is also equally important that once a problem has been identified, practitioners know which professionals to contact. Warning signs include

- age 2–3 – unable to say any words, unable to understand very simple instructions and difficulties with eye-contact;
- age 3–4 – limited number of sounds used, words used are garbled and difficult to interpret, unable to put words together in a coherent way, forgets instructions, unable to respond to questions and has no pragmatic skills and
- age 5+ – constantly switches subject matter when talking or is fixated with one subject, cannot cope with idioms such as 'it's raining cats and dogs' and difficulty learning to read or comprehending.

(Afasic, 2009)

Once a decision has been made to request help from other professionals, it is important to remember that the most fundamental aspect is working *with* the professional and not handing over the problem to the professional. This is at the heart of a true multi-agency approach: working together to support the child and his or her parents and carers in a collaborative way.

Speech and language therapist

Speech and language therapists (SLTs; pronounced 'salt') are usually called when articulation problems have been identified or if a child seems to be struggling with communication. Their role includes assessing the child's speech and language and identifying the difficulty, advising the setting and parents of ways to support the child and assessing the child's progress. There may also be one-to-one therapy sessions. It is important to remember that their role involves working with the adults closest to the child to provide appropriate strategies and an appropriate environment; their work is not just about giving direct support through one-to-one therapy sessions. This aspect of their role is fundamental because there are only a finite number of SLTs in any one area, and therefore, the more parents and practitioners can learn about how they can support their child, the less emphasis there is on the number of one-to-one therapy sessions available. They may also be part of a team of other professionals, including health and social care, which is an example of multi-agency working. SLTs do not only work in educational settings nor do they only work with children. Much of their work also involves working in hospitals and daycare centres and supporting people with physical difficulties, such as difficulty in swallowing or supporting speech after a stroke.

Special Educational Needs Support Service

If a child's problems seem to be in other areas as well as speech and language, such as behaviour and/or learning difficulties, the setting may contact the local authority's Special Educational Needs Support Service. The Code of Practice (DfES, 2001) was established to ensure that providers have a special needs policy and clearly sets out practitioners' responsibilities. These include ensuring that children receive support from outside agencies if the setting has already put internal support systems in place that have not been successful, referred to as Early Years/School Action Plus, and demonstrates an awareness that the child's need is not being met despite different strategies and regular assessments. The support could be from a specialist teacher from the Service or it may be recommended that other professionals could be involved to assess and identify a child's needs, including an educational psychologist, speech therapist or professional from the Behaviour Support Service. It may be that the difficulties with communication and language are part of a wider need that requires specialist support.

Support for children with English as an additional language

If settings have children who do not have English as their first language, then additional support may be necessary. They may have been born in this country but live in homes where the heritage language is mostly spoken or may have only recently arrived into the country. Many of these children will already be very proficient in their first language at a level that is appropriate for their age and may expect to be understood by others. It is important that the professional values the child's heritage language and works in partnership with the parents and the local authority's Ethnic Minority Achievement Service to ensure the practice in the setting is inclusive (DfES/PNS, 2006). Use of gestures, pictures and dual-language signs relating to everyday activities will help communication between the child, the professional and the rest of the children in the setting.

Case study 4

Elka's family arrived in England from Poland 3 weeks ago. This is Elka's first day in the reception class. She does not speak English and seems fairly shy. She smiles at other children and adults and uses occasional Polish words or says nothing. She seems keen to join in playing with the other children, and they enjoy playing with her. She particularly likes the sand and water trays and spends time watching other children playing there as well as playing there herself. No other children or staff speak Polish.

Reflection for early career professional

- What strategies would you put in place to make Elka feel happy and secure?
- What would be the most important things to communicate to her at the beginning?

Reflection for leader/manager

- What policies do you have in place that would support your staff in this situation?
- How would you communicate with Elka's parents?
- What strategies do you have in place or need to put in place to ensure all children feel included, particularly those for whom English is an additional language?

Conclusion

This chapter has highlighted the importance of children communicating effectively to develop as confident, social individuals. The role of adults is crucial in modelling and supporting communication, both verbally and non-verbally. Humans have an intrinsic need to interact with others, and these interactions can have a profound impact on children's confidence and self-esteem. Adults can support and extend children's communication skills in a variety of different ways, and in the early years this should take priority to promote children's progress in all aspects of learning and development. Chapter 2 will consider more specifically how these interactions impact upon children's thinking and learning.

References

Alexander, R. (2004) *Towards Dialogic Teaching: Rethinking Classroom Talk*. York: Dialogos

Afasic (2009) *Lost for Words*. Available from: http://www.afasic.org.uk/pub.htm (Accessed 21 November 2009)

Bentley, L. (2005) *Puppets at Large*. Trowbridge: Positive Press Ltd.

Bowen, C. (1998) *Speech and Language Development in Infants and Young Children*. Available from: http://www.speech-language-therapy.com/devel1.htm (Accessed 4 October 2009)

Bruce, T. (2005) *Early Childhood Education* (3rd edn). Oxon: Hodder Arnold

Bruce, T. and Spratt, J. (2008) *Essentials of Literacy from 0–7*. London: Sage

Bruner, J. (1983) *Child's Talk: Learning to Use Language*. New York: Norton

Chomsky, N (1972) *Language and Mind*. New York: Harcourt Brace Jovanich

Crystal, D. (1995) *The Cambridge Encyclopedia of the English Language*. Cambridge: Cambridge University Press

David, T., Goouch, K., Powell, S. and Abbott, L. (2003) *Birth to Three Matters: A Review of the Literature.* Nottingham: DfES

DCSF (2008) *Setting the Standards for Learning, Development and Care for Children from Birth to Five; Practice Guidance for the Early Years Foundation Stage.* London: DCSF

DfEE (1999) *The National Curriculum: Handbook for Teachers in England.* London: DfEE/QCA

DfES (2001) *Code of Practice on the Identification and Assessment of Children with Special Educational Needs.* London: HMO

DfES/PNS (2006) *Communicating Matters Module 3.* London: DfES

Edwards, C., Gandina, L. and Forman, G. (eds) (1998) *The Hundred Languages of Children.* London: JAI Press

Fiese, B. and Schwartz, M (2008) 'Reclaiming the family table: Mealtimes and child health and wellbeing', in *Social Policy Report* (Volume XXII, Number IV). Available from: http://www.yaleruddcenter.org/resources/upload/docs/what/communities/MealtimeChildHealth.pdf (5 October 2009)

Gasser, M. (2006) *Research Overview of Language Acquisition and Evolution.* Available from: http://www.cs.indiana.edu/~gasser/ (Accessed 24 September 2009)

Goodwin, S. Acredolo, L. and Brown, C. (2000) 'Impact of symbolic gesturing on early language development'. *Journal of Non-Verbal Behaviour*, 24, 81–103

Graddol, D., Cheshire, J. and Swann, J. (1994) *Describing Language.* Buckingham: Open University Press

Grove, N., Herman, R., Morgan, G. and Woll, B. (2004) 'Baby signing: The View from the Sceptics', in *Royal College of Speech and Language Therapists Bulletin.* Available from: http://www.nationaliteracytrust.co.uk (Accessed 25 September 2009)

Herman, R. (2002) *Characteristic Developmental Patterns of Language and Communication in Hearing and Deaf Babies 0–2 Years.* London: Department of Language and Communication, City University

Kisilevsky, B. Hains, S., Lee, K., Xie, X., Huang, H., Ye, H., Khang, K. and Wang, Z. (2003) 'Effects of experience on fetal voice recognition'. *Psychological Science*, 14, (3), 220–224

Lancaster, Y. P. (2003) *Promoting Listening to Young Children – The Reader. Coram Family Listening to Young Children Project.* Maidenhead: Open University Press

Lindon, J. (2005) *Understanding Child Development.* London: Hodder Arnold

Marsh, J. (2005) *Digital Children.* Available from: http://www.open2.net/childofourtime/2005/technology1.html (Accessed 15 September 2009)

Mukherji, P. and O'Dea, T. (2000) *Understanding Children's Language and Literacy.* Cheltenham: Stanley Thornes

National Literacy Trust (2005) *Why Do Many Young Children Lack Basic Language Skills?* Available from: http://www.literacytrust.org.uk/talktoyourbaby/discussionpaper.pdf (Accessed 28 September 2009)

O'Grady, W. (2005) *How Children Use Language.* Cambridge: Cambridge University Press

Skinner, B. F. (1953) *Science and Human Behaviour.* London: Macmillan

Tomasello, M. (2003) *Constructing a Language – A Usage-Based Theory of Language Acquisition.* Harvard University Press

Trevarthen, C. (2008) *Parental Attunement: Sharing Companionship.* Available from: http://www.michaelsieff-foundation.org.uk/content/speechfiles_09_08/trevarthenpdf03.pdf (Accessed 5 October 2009)

Wade, B. and Moore, M. (1998) 'An early start with books: Literacy and mathematical evidence from a longitudinal study'. *Educational Review,* 50, 135–145

Language for Thinking

Introduction

This chapter will consider how children use language to develop their thinking and learning and the ways in which adults can support this development. Language has many purposes, and it is through communication and social interaction that cognitive understanding and development also occur. Among other aspects referred to in the previous chapter, language helps us to

- Examine
- Explain
- Hypothesize
- Reflect
- Analyse
- Argue
- Imagine
- Make connections

- Formulate meanings
- Speculate
- Justify

(Boys, 2008; DfES, 2006; Johnson, 1992)

These cognitive processes and/or purposes for talk need to be nurtured in a supportive context to enable children to organize their understanding of the world (Vygotsky, 1978) in what is known as social constructivism. This support or 'scaffolding' (Bruner, 1983) is a social framework in which adults or peers provide opportunities for learners to internalize and understand an activity by trying out ideas, listening to others and adapting their thinking (Lambirth, 2005). In this way, learning can be consolidated through the use of language and social interaction to articulate understanding. This is not only confined to children. As adults, we often find that by talking out loud we work through problems and consolidate our thinking, whether in a conversation with another person or as a private monologue. This can be as practical as talking through (or arguing!) how to manoeuvre a large piece of furniture through a narrow doorway or as complex as talking through a difficult theoretical idea as a part of our studies. We also use talk to explore our emotions, which has resulted in common sayings such as 'having a shoulder to cry on' or 'a problem shared is a problem halved'. Using the spoken word helps to make thinking a more active process which in turn supports and deepens understanding, clarifies our thoughts and allows us to deal with and make sense of our feelings (Johnston and Nahmad-Williams, 2009).

Language for thinking from birth to 3 years of age

When *Birth to Three Matters* (Sure Start, 2003) was published, there was a component called 'Making Meaning' which highlighted the significance of babies developing a sense of self, a sense of the world around them and a sense of their place in the world. Clearly, this begins with those very early interactions with parents and carers and the close physical and emotional attachments that are formed. Adults closest to the child learn to interpret their baby's cry and respond to different needs, creating routines and rituals around things such as sleeping, bathing and feeding (David et al., 2003). These early rituals are the beginnings of a child's induction into the cultural world in which it lives and from which it will make meaning. They allow children to make predictions and provide them with satisfaction and security when what they thought was going to happen does happen. For example, if bath time is always followed by a story, then this is a ritual that the child expects and feels a sense of security and contentment when it happens. This is referred to as 'intersubjectivity' (Trevarthen, 2008; Wells, 1986), which along with protoconversations (see Chapter 1) involves the mutual attention of adult and child, which is essential to communication and learning. The adult and child are sharing a ritual of bath time and story, and both benefit from the closeness of the interactions that occur during this ritual. The early social interactions in the first few months, such as smiling and reaching out, are the baby's way of both communicating meaning and constructing meaning.

As speech develops, the enjoyment of playing with sounds, experimenting with words and discovering the rules and structures of language are also examples of children learning about themselves as individuals within their culture. They often take the initiative in their conversations and take charge and direct, even though their spoken language may still be limited (David et al., 2003; Maclure, 1992). They may indicate they want a toy and what they want the adult to do with the toy or may indicate they want a book and when they are tired of the story in that book they want another. The adults' talk with the child is described in terms of four Ss by Maclure (1992): shaping, sharing, supporting and stretching. The shaping is done in the early stages through use of infant-directed speech and repetition such as repeating sounds or words the child uses (see Chapter 1). Sharing is the mutual recognition of shared experiences and talking through these experiences and feelings, such as sharing a book or going for a walk and talking about what you see. Supporting is understanding the child's developmental level and not expecting too much or too little, such as accepting a child's shyness with a new adult and not forcing interactions which would make the child feel uncomfortable. Finally, stretching is creating conditions that allow the child to develop, which is what Vygotsky (1978) termed the zone of proximal development where the adult or peer helps the child to go further than would have been possible on his or her own. This could be the introduction of new vocabulary, helping with articulation or questioning and discussing to develop an idea.

Case study 1

Alfie is 3 months old and Emily is 2 years and 1 month old. They are with their mother in the kitchen, and Alfie is being breastfed at the kitchen table. Emily is stroking Alfie's head and talking.

Emily: (singing) Happy birthday to you.

Mum: It isn't Alfie's birthday yet!

Emily: Me birthday girl.

Mum: Yes you're a big girl now – how old are you?

Emily: Two. Alfie's two (laughing).

Mum: Alfie isn't two – he's a baby. (Gently to Alfie, looking into his eyes and stroking his face) Aren't you sweetheart – yes, yes. (Making sucking noises) Is that nice? Mmmmm? You are a hungry boy.

Emily: (Getting a book) Look! That's a rabbit. (Turning the pages) That's a pig. That's a seep. (Mum is rocking Alfie and gently humming but looking at the book with Emily, nodding when she names an animal in the picture)

Mum: Yes. Sheep.

Emily: That's a cow. That's a bird.

Mum: What sort of bird?

Emily: Carrot.

Mum: (laughing) Nearly! It's a parrot.

Emily: It's a carrot parrot. T'eats carrots.

Mum: I don't think parrots eat carrots, Emmy.

Emily: Yeh – eat carrots. Carrot parrot.

Mum: Oh it's a carrot parrot is it?

Emily: Yes (laughing). Carrot parrot carrot parrot.

Reflection for early career professional

- What examples can you see of the four Ss: shaping, sharing, supporting and stretching?
- Consider who is directing and controlling the conversation. Why do you think this is?

Reflection for leader/manager

- Can you observe and provide examples of adults using the four Ss, shaping, sharing, supporting and stretching, in your setting?
- When observing child/adult conversations in your setting, who tends to direct and control the conversation? If the balance is towards the adult, how can you shift that balance so that the child is the initiator and director?

Key research in the 1980s (Tizard and Hughes, 1984; Wells, 1986) indicated that talk in the home was more extensive than in the nursery setting and involved 'the cumulative and collaborative construction of meaning' (Wells, 1986: 47). There are clearly logistical reasons why this might be in terms of adult/child ratios, but it does raise the issue of the need for practitioners to be aware of children's prior experiences and to provide opportunities for children to initiate, lead and extend conversations at their own level and in their own time. In the early stages, this can happen before speech is developed. A child minder was looking after a 12-month-old child called Ruby and she had a basket of lids on the floor. Ruby took one lid and the child minder also took a lid. Ruby then took another lid and banged them together, followed by the child minder who did the same thing. This copying continued until Ruby banged her lid against a lid the child minder was holding. This 'conversation' was initiated and led by Ruby, allowing her to explore and learn at her own pace. This same principle can be adopted in verbal interactions, not by copying in the same way, but by allowing the child to take the lead and respond rather than direct or dominate.

Vygotsky (1978) believed that, alongside physical exploration, speech allowed children to make meaning and sense of the world. He believed that thought and language were interlinked and that thoughts were not merely expressed in words but were formed and shaped through words. As children develop speech they are able to organize and structure new concepts through language (Lambirth, 2005). Speech can give labels to new concepts, such as a child learning that not all large animals are cows when calling a horse a cow on seeing it for the first time and then being introduced to the new word 'horse'. This is developing the child's understanding of animals. Although labelling new concepts is one aspect of language and thought, it is far more complex than that. Words without thought are empty and meaningless. A baby's first word is not really considered a word unless meaning can be attributed to it. 'Dada' is just a sound unless the baby uses it in the context that gives it meaning, for example, when seeing daddy, wanting daddy or hearing daddy. As a child becomes a more competent speaker, more complex thoughts can be shaped through language. This is why it is essential for practitioners to view language development as cognitive, as well as social, development.

Language for thinking from 3 to 5 years of age

As stated in Chapter 1, children are now becoming very competent language users and can manipulate language in different contexts. Early language tends to be rooted in the immediate context, corresponding with what the child is doing or what the child wants. As children get older they can refer to past events or speculate about future events. They are also able to make connections between similar experiences or ideas. Through talk children show their ability to express their feelings, respond to others, take turns, further their own learning and assume joint responsibility for establishment of meaning and for a range of purposes (Maclure, 1992). They use language to

- Recount
- Describe
- Request
- Offer directions
- Ask questions
- Explain
- Argue
- Instruct
- Speculate
- Tell a story

Case study 2

Two boys talking at nursery

K: I went to the fair and went on a . . . on a . . . it went round and round.
P: Did it? Round and round?
K: Yeh. Round and round and I went on it.
P: I went on swing.

⇨

Case study—Cont'd

K: No, no there isn't a swing.

P: I did. In the park. It swinged.

K: No, the fair. The fair's big with loads of rides and . . . scary. I went on them. Whoosh. Up and down and . . . and . . . I went really, really, really fast. You got to hold on like this or you fall off. I couldn't go on some cos I'm not big enough. They have a thing you stand on to see if you can go . . . be big. A measure thing like in my bedroom. You stand at it.

P: Can I come?

K: No. I been now. Maybe you could come next time. I'll ask my dad. I think – don't know if we go again. He might let you.

P: Yeh. I come.

Reflection for early career professional

- How many different uses of language can you identify from those listed earlier?
- What does the children's use of language tell you about their ability to make connections?

Reflection for leader/manager

- Consider children's and adults' use of language in your setting based on the list given earlier. Do any dominate?
- Notice when children talk about things that are not related to the immediate context. What sort of connections are they making? What does this tell you about their learning?

Children's conversations with each other can provide a wealth of opportunities for social and cognitive development. The relaxed atmosphere created when children are playing and talking together allows children to 'lead their own intellectual search' (Lindon, 2005: 176). There is often a tendency for practitioners to feel pressured to step in and try and promote a learning opportunity when if children are left alone they do it by themselves. That is not to say that adults do not have a role to play, but it is important to know when to

Photograph 2.1 Children playing and talking (photograph by Emma Jordan)

join in by listening and then contributing to a real conversation rather than jumping in with questions and prompts.

Sustained shared thinking is a term used by Siraj-Blatchford et al. (2002) to describe the intellectual interaction between adults and children or children and children on a one-to-one or small group basis. I am using the term intellectual here to mean working together to solve a problem, evaluate an experience, define a concept or explore ideas. It involves the adult really tuning in to the child, showing a genuine interest and respecting the child's ideas. These conversations are excellent examples of language for thinking and give the adult a wonderful insight into the child's thoughts and developing concepts and understanding of the world.

Case study 3

The teacher had been out pond dipping with two boys from the reception class. They had returned to the classroom with some water snails in their bucket. They also had some garden snails in a tank in the classroom.

⇨

Case study—Cont'd

Teacher: Let's look at these pond snails and see if they are the same as the garden snails.

Tom: No they are not.

Rav: They are – they've both got shells.

Teacher: Yes that's true. I think all snails have shells.

Tom: Yeh – if they don't then it's a slug.

Rav: The pond snail has got a curly shell.

Tom: It sort of twirly and pointy.

Rav: Like an ice cream.

Teacher: Oh yes! It's like an ice cream cone. The garden snails' shells aren't – I wonder how we could describe their shell.

Tom: Flat and sort of twirly.

Rav: It's a spiral and it's grey and stripey but the pond snail is dark and I can't see any stripes.

Teacher: Yes, a flat spiral is a good description. I think maybe the water is making the pond snail look dark. What do you think?

Tom: Don't know. My hair looks dark when it's wet.

Rav: Mine looks the same.

Teacher: Well yours is dark anyway, Ravi. The garden snails definitely have different shells.

Ravi: Can garden snails live in water?

Teacher: I don't know. Is there a way we could find out?

Tom: We could put them in the water and see.

Teacher: Well we could but . . . (the teacher doesn't finish the sentence).

Tom: No! It might die.

Rav: It might drown. We mustn't hurt it. We have to put it back in the garden soon.

Teacher: That's true, Ravi. We mustn't hurt it. We will put it back in the garden soon. I think we all agree that we mustn't put it in water.

Ravi: No.

Tom: I think if garden snails could live in water they would go in water so maybe they can't.

Teacher: Yes, Tom, I think you could be right there. I've never seen a garden snail in a pond.

Ravi: Like fish. Fish die if they're not in water.

⇨

Reflection for early career professional

Consider the following uses of language and identify if and when the teacher uses these:

- Asking open questions (What might happen if? I wonder why? What do you think?).
- Suggesting (we could try . . .; maybe it's because . . .).
- Affirming (that's a good idea).
- Recapping (so you think that . . .).
- Reciprocating (I agree; I like that too).
- Clarifying (Okay, so we won't do that because you think that . . .).
- Challenging (I don't agree; Are you sure?) or offering an alternative suggestion (Maybe it won't happen like that, maybe it will . . .).
- Speculating (Do you think it would be like that if . . .?).

Reflection for leader/manager

- How do you provide opportunities for sustained shared thinking when you have a large number of children with only one or two adults?
- Consider ways of supporting your staff in developing their ability to engage in this type of conversation with small groups or on a one-to-one basis.

The different types of language use are often described as 'strategies' in various books and websites, but I think that they are actually the features of a natural conversation. It is perhaps more tentative than an adult-to-adult conversation in the sense that the teacher is less forthright in voicing his or her views to allow the child to formulate ideas, but otherwise it follows the natural pathway of a conversation. Rather than trying to introduce these as 'strategies' to support teachers, we really need to just move away from the question and answer format that is traditionally associated with the teacher/pupil relationship and move towards a mutually enhancing conservation. As with any conversation, there is more potential if there is a good relationship between the participants and there is trust and mutual respect. For successful sustained shared thinking to take place, the development of positive, trusting relationships between practitioners and children is essential.

Narrative

A child's world is full of stories: from the narratives of everyday events, such as a parent telling the story of the day 'We're going to get dressed and have our breakfast and then we are going to walk to the park to feed the ducks' or recapping an event, to being told stories or experiencing stories in books, on television or on the computer. Stories help us to shape our understanding and children make sense of their world by constructing stories. 'Narrative is central to the operation of the human mind' (Grainger, 1997: 34) or, in the often quoted words of Hardy (1977: 13), 'Narrative is the primary act of mind'. The main point is that we think in narrative and use this narrative to gain understanding. We search for meaning though narrative. If you think of dreams you may have had, the more bizarre and disjointed they are, the more disturbing they appear. We can't find a narrative pathway through and this confuses us. We make connections through narrative and learn to interpret our experiences and feelings. If you think about a typical day, you think about it in terms of a story and often communicate these stories to other people, such as the horrendous journey into work or the overheard amusing conversation on the train. Stories, such as anecdotes, help us to contextualize things. Children are full of their own anecdotes about their lives and imaginary stories that they tell through play. Through stories that children hear, they can relate to feelings within their experience and learn about things outside their own experience. Wells (1986) highlights the importance of listening to and creating stories to make meaning: 'To try to make sense, to construct stories, and to share them with others in speech and in writing is an essential part of being human' (Wells, 1986: 222).

There is a recognized developmental sequence in the way children begin to use and communicate narrative. As soon as children notice something and want to communicate this to others, they are beginning to use narrative. Once children can use two- or three-word sentences (see Chapter 1), their use of narrative develops significantly.

The development of narrative

Nine to twenty-four months

Nine months onwards, children will vocalize, look, or point at something to show the adult that they are interested in it. For example, they will point at a toy to tell the adult that they want it. They will look at the adult they are trying to communicate with and then back at the toy. At 12 months onwards children will be able to show an understanding of an occurrence that has just happened by making a response to it, such as referring to a television programme just after it has been turned off by using a character's name or imitating a sound made on the programme or in the theme tune.

Two years

Children refer to things that have happened to them and they are usually supported by the adult. Initially, they may only mention one event that has happened quite recently, such as going to the park. They then start to refer to more detail and will refer to more than one event by talking about seeing the ducks and going on the swing. From this stage onwards, narratives are a natural part of children's conversations. Adults can support this by providing prompts, asking questions and joining in with the narrative as part of a two-way conversation and shared experience, such as 'wasn't it funny when the duck's bottom stuck up out of the water . . .'

Three to four years

When 3 years old, children are able to talk about places and do so more than talking about people. They may not be able to sequence the events in the correct order and they do leave out some significant information. As children get older, they remember more detail and they are able to link events together. For example, they may say 'we ate our picnic and then we went to feed the ducks with the sandwiches we had left'. There tends to be an emphasis on 'and then' as the way to link events, rather than using more complex connectives.

Five to six years

Children are able to talk about where and when something happened and they refer to the people involved, including reference to emotions. They recognize cause and effect and will often structure their story around a problem and the resulting consequences. For example, 'When we went to feed the ducks, Auntie Jane came and she was scared of the duck when it started quacking and walking up to her. She was scared and ran away! Me and mummy were laughing because she looked funny. She was all right though. The ducks just wanted her bread but she got scared. I'm not scared of ducks so I stayed and fed them.'

Children are also aware of story structure and characters from the stories that have been read to them. They understand conventional evil and good characters and can begin to structure their own stories using the conventions of story, such as a problem that needs to be solved.

Adapted from TDA (2008, Session 9: 47)

Storytelling

Telling stories, rather than reading stories, is an excellent way of communicating with children. The eye contact, response to children's facial expressions and body language and use of gesture draws the children into the world of the story. It is a truly interactive experience that allows the storyteller to adapt the story depending on the reactions of the audience. The many beautiful picture books that are available have possibly resulted in more story reading than storytelling, but we must try to ensure that we maintain this oral tradition that is present in every culture.

Case study 4

The students on the BA (Hons) Primary Education with QTS programme at Bishop Grosseteste University College Lincoln take part in a storytelling event during the first few weeks of their course. They go to a local primary school and are paired with a child. They get to know their child's interests and then go back to college and write a story for their child with a view to telling, not reading, the story. They then create a storytelling environment which reflects the theme of the story. For example, stories about princes and princesses might be told in a castle or stories about football on a football pitch, all created with imagination and lots of material, cardboard and paint. The students practise their stories and often make props to support the telling of the story. The children then come into college for a storytelling day where they listen to the stories created for them and take part in related activities. The students are always extremely nervous before the event and feel a great sense of achievement at the end of the day. This experience is one that is most often quoted by students as one of the most significant on the 3-year course.

Reflection for early career professional

- What sorts of skills do you think the students will be practising during the preparation and completion of the storytelling event?
- How might these skills be transferred into the classroom?

⇨

Reflection for leader/manager

- What would be the advantages of organizing a similar event with your staff in your setting?
- How would you support staff in increasing the numbers of stories told rather than read?

Practical task 2.1

Prepare a traditional story to tell to a group of children and then evaluate its success. Prepare your own story to tell to a group of children. Include props and sound effects if you feel they would enhance the experience. Consider the following:

- How will you decide on the genre and content of the story?
- How will you structure it?
- How much audience participation would you expect?
- What strategies will you use to help you remember the story?

After telling your stories, consider what you and the children gained from the experience. Compare this with reading a story and consider the benefits and drawbacks of both.

Playing

Children create stories through play. It is their world in which they have control and feel confident to explore ideas and feelings. Children's expressive language is often very rich when they are playing as they experiment with narrative and characters. They take on different roles and create new situations or recreate situations from their own experiences. When I was teaching in a reception class, I would often hear my own voice coming out of 4-year-old Lottie's mouth as she organized a small group of children to sit on the carpet while she took the register. It was quite unnerving to see how she replicated my way of sitting and vocal inflections to the closest detail! Children are also very

Photograph 2.2 Retelling a story (photograph by Emma Jordan)

adept at switching in and out of role and being true to the role they have created. Gemma, who was 2 and a half years old, was playing with her mother. She had decided that she would be the 'mum' and her mother would be the baby. As they were playing, Gemma fell and bumped her knee. As she started to cry she said 'I'm not mummy anymore, I'm Gemma, and I can cry because I've hurt my knee.' Gemma was demonstrating an understanding of her role during the play and her subsequent need for comfort, which meant clearly stating that she had reverted back to Gemma and needed a cuddle.

Children often recreate stories that they have heard. Familiar traditional stories that have a clear structure, such as 'Little Red Riding Hood' and 'Goldilocks and the Three Bears' have a distinct narrative, repetition and well-known phrases that children are able to use. These stories give children a sense of control and security as they know what is going to happen next.

Providing children with props or puppets can help to enhance the experience, but too much direction will inhibit the play experience. Allow the children freedom of choice and freedom of expression by providing time, space and accessible resources and leaving the children to play. Bruce and Spratt (2008) suggest that research indicates that children who do not have sufficient opportunities to explore narrative and characters through play make less progress in reading and writing. Exploring narratives through play certainly helps children to make connections between the spoken and written word and making connections is a vital cognitive process to develop understanding.

The world of media is often very significant in children's lives, and children's play will often reflect what they have seen on television or films. Popular culture is very familiar to the majority of children and can provide a similar sense of control and security that traditional tales provide. Marsh (1999) describes a role-play area that was turned into Batman's and Batwoman's headquarters, which proved very popular with all the children. What was significant was the number of boys who chose to play in the role-play area who usually avoided going into the area and the girls were just as interested as the boys. Using narratives and characters from the media also provides links between home and school. What is paramount is that children are motivated to explore characters and narratives through play, whether the stimuli is a story from a book, an imaginary story, a real life experience or a story from television or film.

Transition to Key Stage 1 (5 to 7 years of age)

As children move from the reception class to KS1, opportunities for sustained free play are often reduced. The emphasis tends to be on literacy rather than oracy although most practitioners do acknowledge the value of talk on learning. The main difference is that the talk tends to be promoted in more formal situations. There are specific times set aside for children to talk, such as 'show and tell'-type activities, circle time, talk partners and some group work, but the significance of language for thinking is not always apparent (Alexander, 2004).

Case study 5

A year 1 class is having a story at the end of the day. The story is finished and there are 5 minutes left; so, the teacher asks if anyone has brought anything to show. Abby puts up her hand and says she has brought her certificate. The teacher asks her to get it.

Teacher: So Abby, what's this (holding the certificate).
Abby: My certificate.
Teacher: And what did you get this for?
Abby: Dancing.
Teacher: Dancing? Oh very good. What did you have to dance?
Abby: Erm . . .
Teacher: Is it for one dance that you did?
Abby: Er . . . no.
Teacher: For lots of dancing?
   Abby nods.
Teacher: Well that's very clever Abby. You must be a very good dancer. You'll have to show us some of your dancing one day. Isn't she clever? Shall we give her a clap?
   The class clap and Abby smiles shyly.
Teacher: Right, well, you needn't put it away because it's time to get our coats for home time in a minute. Go and sit down.

Reflection for early career professional

- What do you think was the purpose of this 'show and tell'?
- Abby was clearly proud of her certificate and wanted to share her success. Think of different ways for Abby to have done this that might have encouraged her to lead the talking and have control.

Reflection for leader/manager

- Do you recognize this situation in your setting? If so, how might things be done differently to allow the child to have control and lead the talking? If not, what do you do to celebrate children's achievements or encourage them to share things they have done at home?
- What are your views on 'show and tell'? Think of different ways that 'show and tell' could be organized to reduce the input from the teacher.

Small group work

The importance of group work and a dialogic approach to teaching was discussed in Chapter 1. In this chapter, we will focus more on how group work allows children to engage in sustained talk that is the next step on from sustained shared thinking. Through shared talk children can clarify ideas, challenge others, internalize meaning and develop understanding (Logue and Smith, 2007). Shared talk depends less on the adult than sustained shared thinking and more on the support of peers. The teacher observes and visits the groups, but keeps any input to a minimum. The onus is on the children and relies on their relationship rather than the authority of the teacher to scaffold the discussions.

Logue and Smith (2007) acknowledge that many teachers feel uncomfortable with the idea of small group work and shared talk because of fears that children are too young to cooperate without the teacher, worries about noise and behaviour and anxiety about time within the constraints of the curriculum. It is important to remember that children have already demonstrated their ability to play together for sustained periods and therefore are capable of working together as a group. We need to ensure they are clear about the characteristics of effective group work, as outlined in Chapter 1, and may need more guidance and coaching in the early stages. Clear planning, careful grouping and purposeful tasks should help to allay fears about noise and behaviour, although any activity that involves talk must result in some level of noise. Using group work as part of the speaking and listening curriculum or as a cross-curricular approach should address issues about ensuring the curriculum is being met.

Strategies that help to make the tasks purposeful include the following:

- Selecting from options – the children could be given a range of foods, which they need to choose from for a 4-year-old's birthday party menu.
- Prioritizing options – the children are given a range of different playground equipment and have to choose three in order of importance giving reasons for their choices.
- Comparing items against criteria – children are given a list of criteria for books that the next class needs (only books about animals, some fiction and non-fiction, some

with photos, at least five different animals included in the selection). They then have to compare the books given to the criteria and make the selection.

- Analysing scenarios – the children are told a story about a family who want a pet with their likes and dislikes and they then decide what pet they should have. (Adapted from Logue and Smith, 2007: 30, based on Howe, 1997)

It is important that the children have something to work towards and know that there is an end product although it is actually the process that provides the opportunities for learning. Giving time limits can also help to focus the discussion and helps children to organize their talk. It is also useful for children to have resources that they can touch and move to help to keep their interest and to aid the discussion. The teacher's main role is to plan the activity carefully so that it is not so open that the discussion loses direction or so obvious that very little talk is required to complete the task. If the tasks are based on the topics being taught then it gives the discussion a purposeful context, aids the application of recently acquired knowledge and supports developing understanding.

Practical task 2.2

Plan a task for small group work based on one of the examples provided and observe the children. Evaluate how it went in terms of children's talk for thinking rather than the outcome.

Reflection for early career professional

- If you were to do this again what would you do the same and what would you do differently?
- How would you assess children's learning and what are the practical implications?

Reflection for leader/manager

- How do you ensure small group work is purposeful in your setting?
- What strategies would you put in place to support practitioners in planning successful small group work sessions?

Case study 6

Snowballing

The children were discussing the party games they wanted at the Christmas party and needed to choose three. The teacher organized the children into pairs and after 5 minutes of discussion joined pairs together to make groups of four. After another few minutes, she asked the groups to combine to make eight in each group to finish the discussion.

Rainbowing

The children are in 'home' groups of equal size (five in a group). Each child in each group is given a colour and the colours then form separate groups so that the children from each group who have been given red form a new 'red' group, those given yellow form a new 'yellow' group, etc. The task for each colour group is to design a logo for the school sweatshirt. After 20 minutes, the children re-form into their home groups and each member (each having been in a different colour group) discusses what their logo will look like and why.

Jigsawing

The children are in home groups and have been asked to re-design the classroom. Each member of the group is given a different area, for example role-play area, book corner area, wet area, etc. New 'expert' groups are formed based on the area, for example a role-play group, a book corner group, etc. After discussions, the members of the 'expert' groups go back into home groups and share their ideas.

Reflection for early career professional

- What might be the advantages and disadvantages of the different ways the groups have been organized?
- Can you think of other examples for the different groupings?

Reflection for leader/manager

- Does your setting use different grouping methods? If so, what are the advantages and what are the issues? If not, how might you introduce this?
- In staff meetings, how do you ensure that everyone has a chance to work with someone different or have their say about an issue?

Conclusion

Although children are becoming more skilful readers and writers in KS1 we must not underestimate the role of talk to underpin understanding. The conversations that go alongside reading support children's comprehension and provide a valuable shared experience. It also provides children with experience of the written word, which will have an impact on their own writing. The talk that goes before writing is vital in enabling children to clarify ideas, make connections and provide the necessary foundations to support children in developing their own writing. Although the rest of this book is focusing on developing literacy skills, we cannot overemphasize the essential role of talk in the development of literacy.

References

Alexander, R. (2004) *Towards Dialogic Teaching: Rethinking Classroom Talk.* York: Dialogos

Boys, R. (2008) 'Communication, language and literacy', in Basford, J. and Hodson, E. (eds) *Teaching Early Years Foundation Stage.* Exeter: Learning Matters, pp. 67–84

Bruce, T. and Spratt, J. (2008) *Essentials of Literacy from 0–7.* London: Sage

Bruner, J. (1983) *Child's Talk: Learning to Use Language.* New York: Norton

David, T., Goouch, K., Powell, S. and Abbott, L. (2003) *Birth to Three Matters: A Review of the Literature.* Nottingham: DfES

DfES (2006) *Communicating Matters: Module 2.* London: DfES

Grainger, T. (1997) *Traditional Storytelling in the Primary Classroom.* Leamington Spa: Scholastic

Hardy, B. (1977) 'Narrative as a primary act of mind', in Meek, M., Warlow, A. and Barton, G. (eds) *The Cool Web, the Pattern of Children's Reading.* London: Bodley Head, pp. 12–23

Howe, A. (1997) *Making Talk Work.* Sheffield: Hodder and Stoughton

Johnson, J. (1992) 'Some unanswered questions about the development and assessment of talk in the secondary years', in Norman, K. (ed.) *Thinking Voices: The Work of the National Oracy Project.* London: Hodder and Stoughton, pp. 50–60

Johnston, J. and Nahmad-Williams, L. (2009) *Early Childhood Studies.* Harlow: Pearson Education

Lambirth, A. (2005) *Reflective Reader Primary English.* Exeter: Learning Matters

Lindon, J. (2005) *Understanding Child Development.* London: Hodder Arnold

Logue, J. and Smith, V. (2007) 'Group talk in the early years', in Cremin, T. and Dombey, H. (eds) *Handbook of Primary English in Initial Teacher Education.* Cambridge: UKLA/NATE

Maclure, M. (1992) 'The first five years: The development of talk in the pre-school period', in Norman, K. (ed.) *Thinking Voices: The Work of the National Oracy Project.* London: Hodder and Stoughton, pp. 16–26

Marsh, J. (1999) 'Telly tubby tales: Popular culture and media education', in Marsh, J. and Hallet, E. (eds) *Desirable Literacies.* London: Paul Chapman, pp. 153–174

Siraj-Blatchford, I., Sylva, K., Muttock, S., Gilden, R. and Bell, D. (2002) *Researching Effective Pedagogy in the Early Years*. Nottingham: DfES

Sure Start (2003) *Birth to Three Matters*. London: DfES

TDA (2008) *Special Educational Needs and/or Disabilities Training Resource for Initial Teacher Training Providers*. London: TDA

Tizard, B. and Hughes, M. (1984) *Young Children Learning: Talking and Thinking at Home and at School*. London: Fontana

Vygotsky, L. (1978) *Thought and Language*. Cambridge, MA: MIT Press

Wells, G. (1986) *The Meaning Makers*. London: Hodder and Stoughton

Linking Sounds and Letters

Introduction

The importance of children learning to read and write with confidence and skill to function effectively within a literate society is not under debate. However, the way we teach and support children in the development of their reading and writing is a contentious issue and continues to attract different viewpoints and arguments. Lockwood (1996) lists a range of approaches to reading, including phonics, look and say, real books and language experience as specific methods that are often used in isolation. Merchant (1999) suggests that these bottom–up (skills based, starting with letters) or top–down (meaning based, starting with content) approaches to reading are not as distinct from one another as has been suggested. It appears then that within the arguments about which method to use, there are also differences of opinion about how these methods are used. Although writing does not tend to receive the same level of media attention as reading in terms of standards, there are also a range of different viewpoints about the teaching of writing, particularly in terms of the emphasis on either the process of writing or the end product (Whitehead, 1990). Whatever the argument, few would disagree with the importance of speaking and listening as a precursor and partner to reading and writing and the ability to link sounds and letters.

The phonics debate

The EYFS (DCSF, 2008) uses the phrase 'Linking Sounds and Letters' rather than 'phonics', although they both mean virtually the same thing. The teaching and learning of phonics involves letter/sound correspondence, also known as grapheme/phoneme correspondence (GPC), to aid reading and writing (Johnston and Nahmad-Williams, 2009). Perhaps the reason the word 'phonics' was not used is because of the strong views held about phonics in terms of whether and how it should be taught and the quite legitimate fear that a formal approach to reading and writing would be taken by professionals in a way that is inappropriate for young children.

Hall (1987) believes in the importance of emergent reading, based on the work of Goodman (1980) in Hall (1987), in which children become readers naturally through exposure to print and a supportive environment and through an intrinsic search for meaning. This view does not agree with systematic, non-contextual instruction associated with phonics teaching. Many of the books about early reading printed in the past 40 years place greater emphasis on the importance of sharing books and context than on the more skill-based approach linked to phonics. Whitehead (2009: 123) states that the teaching of phonics 'runs counter to the spirit of the core principles' in the EYFS (DCSF, 2008), which emphasizes the significance of play and the development of the unique child. There is, however, a widely held belief that phonics teaching is very beneficial to the development of reading (Boys, 2008; DfES, 2006a; Wray and Medwell, 2008), but even within this shared belief, there are differences of opinion on how phonics should be approached. Before outlining these differences, it must be stressed that phonics should be part of a much broader approach to the development of reading and writing. This includes rich speaking and listening opportunities, access to a wide range of print, sharing books and reading and writing opportunities in play. Chapters 4 and 5 will focus more specifically on the range of approaches used to develop reading and writing.

Analytic and synthetic phonics

Terminology

- Phoneme: the smallest unit of sound, for example 'f'.
- Grapheme: the written representation of a phoneme, for example fish and photo.
- Digraph: two letters representing one phoneme, for example 'ch' or 'ee'.
- Phonological awareness: being able to hear different sounds within words.

Linking sounds and letters is basically linking phonemes and graphemes.

The two main types of phonics mostly discussed are analytic phonics and synthetic phonics. Analytic phonics tends to focus on common attributes in whole words. Words beginning with the same letter and sound will be grouped together, for example, ball, boat, Billy, banana and boots. The common sequence then leads to identifying words with the same final sound, for example cat, sit and met, and then to those with the same medial sound, for example, cat, can and rat. Goswami (1995) discusses the impact of children's awareness of onset and rime on their reading, which means identifying those words that have the same end unit, for example cat, hat and sat or hard, card and lard. Analytic phonics is based on sounds being identified within whole words to provide analogies with new words. This means that if a child knows the word 'look' and needs to read or spell the word 'book', a straight-forward link can be made. Wray and Medwell (2008) and Johnston and Watson (2007) both cite the criticisms of analytic phonics, with particular emphasis on the slow introduction of the GPC. This is typified by the common 'letter of the week' displays that were often seen in early years classrooms.

The Review of Early Reading chaired by Jim Rose (DfES, 2006a) states that there is overwhelming evidence to suggest that the synthetic approach to phonics is the most effective approach, although Wray and Medwell (2008) and Goouch and Lambirth (2007) urge caution in accepting the rather narrow research evidence based on a small study of 300 children in Scotland. The synthetic approach teaches children a few letter sounds to enable them to start blending straight away and continues to teach new sounds at a rapid rate (Johnston and Watson, 2007). They are introduced to sounds rather than words and then learn to blend these sounds to make words. For example, they are introduced to the sounds 's', 'a' and 't' as separate phonemes and then blend them together to make the word 'at' or 'sat'. The 'Letters and Sounds' publication (PNS/DfES, 2007) is based on the synthetic approach and has been adopted by many primary schools in England. This is the approach the government recommends, although the Letter and Sounds programme is only one of many phonics schemes available. Boys (2008) and Dombey (1999) firmly believe that both analytic phonics and synthetic phonics should be taught together as they complement one another, whereas advocates of each system cite their approach is the most effective and should be taught exclusively.

It is unlikely that there will ever be a consensus of opinion about phonics, and experts will continue to debate many of the issues related to the development of reading and writing. As professionals working with young children, it is important that we understand children's developmental stages and the essential role of speaking and listening in developing children's awareness of the sounds in their language and how these link to reading and writing.

Linking sounds and letters from birth to 3 years of age

Babies are alert to noise and recognize their mother's voice and familiar sounds. They enjoy playing with the sounds they can make with their voice and lips. They repeat sounds such as 'aba aba', whisper, squeal, gurgle, growl and blow bubbles. As they get a little older they may experiment with repeated sounds by changing the vowel, such as 'digga doo, digga day', and try new sounds by running their fingers over their lips. Singing to babies, talking, laughing, making noises and whispering all provide a range of different sounds in rhythm, pitch and dynamics. Many toys have sounds and babies soon learn how to create the noise through banging, shaking, squeezing, pressing or winding. Walks outside provide a wealth of sounds from those made by people such as footsteps and talking, those made by animals and birds, those made by traffic or machinery and general sounds in the environment, such as the wind rustling leaves. Many homes are filled with sounds from the buzzing of the fridge, water boiling in a kettle, television, computer, radio and music systems. Babies soon begin to differentiate between these sounds, and this skill is vital if they are to develop phonological awareness as they grow older.

Case study 1

Jessica, aged 3 months, was being held by her mother and was joined by her father and auntie. The three adults began to sing to a song that was on the radio and Jessica's mother danced with Jessica in her arms. Jessica made a range of sounds from quite deep throaty grunting sounds to high-pitched squealing. She also made dolphin-like noises that she hadn't made before.

Jessica was in her musical rocking chair. She sat happily, looking in the mirror and listening to the music. She began to jig her upper body and banged her hand against the dangling toys. She enjoyed making the toys rattle and continued to bang her hand against them for sometime.

Reflection for early career professional

- Consider the songs you sing with children. How do you ensure that you include a wide variety of songs in terms of rhythm and pitch?
- What types of resources do you have that allow babies and young children to make a variety of noises with different objects on their own?
- Observe babies making sounds with different objects and note what interests them and what they do to make the sounds.

Reflection for leader/manager

- Consider the environment in your setting. Can you list a range of activities and resources that allow children to listen to and explore sounds?
- Which of these activities can be done independently and which are shared with other children and adults? Why are both important?

Songs that include different noises help to develop sound discrimination. 'Old Macdonald Had a Farm' or 'I am the Music Man' provide children with opportunities to join in with the different sounds even if they can't join in with the words. Nursery rhymes and tongue twisters are full of repetitive sounds and rhymes. Children may begin to develop their own little rhymes through word play, which demonstrates that they are able to discriminate between sounds and create their own. They also enjoy singing or saying well-known one-line rhymes such as 'easy peasy lemon squeazy', 'see you later alligator' or 'night night, sleep tight'. Many picture books include repetition, rhyme and

Photograph 3.1 Children saying rhymes (Photography by L Nahmd-Williams)

alliteration, which encourage joining in and prediction. The more children hear and say rhymes, the more they will become aware of the different sounds in words, which will promote their phonological awareness.

Linking sounds and letters from 3 to 5 years of age

As children's speaking and listening skills become more developed, activities can be planned more specifically to link sounds with words. It is important that this does not happen before a child is able to identify different sounds in words. I had a child in my reception class who did not know his colours and I would often hear the other children try to help him. They would use crayons and would attempt to give him a clue by holding a red crayon and saying "What colour is this Jason? It's 'r' 'rrr' 'rrr' . . ." to which Jason would reply, "'rrr' 'rrr' blue!" Not only was it clear that Jason did not know his colours, but it was also clear that he could not differentiate letter sounds or link individual sounds to sounds in words. Until children can hear and say individual sounds it is inappropriate, and frankly a waste of time, to try and make GPC.

Phonological awareness

Johnston and Watson (2007: 14) state that a synthetic phonics programme develops phonemic awareness without needing to be 'preceded by a phoneme awareness training programme'. I agree that a phonemic awareness 'training programme' is not appropriate and sounds very formal and regimented. I firmly believe that unless children have had a range of opportunities to explore sound in their play and through rhymes and singing they will struggle to discriminate sounds in our language. The development of phonological awareness is a crucial first step in phonics teaching and is the first phase in Letters and Sounds (PNS/DfES, 2007). I believe this is a particular strength of Letters and Sounds, as it clearly advocates the need for well-developed phonological awareness before moving onto more systematic phonics teaching. It is worth noting that any child with hearing difficulties or articulation difficulties will find this more difficult and it could affect later reading and spelling. A common example of this is a child who cannot make a 'th' sound and substituting it with a 'v' sound, spelling 'with' as 'wiv' or 'this' as 'vis'.

Activities that promote listening include going on a sound walk and identifying the sounds that can be heard; identifying recorded sounds; playing sounds behind a screen and asking the children to identify the instrument being used; using voices to help a child find a hidden toy by going louder when the child is near the toy or quieter when the child is far from the toy. Activities that promote the use of sounds include putting different toy animals into a bag and asking the children to make the noise of each animal as it is pulled out of the bag; adding sound effects to stories; singing songs or saying rhymes in different types of voices, such as very high or low voice, fast or slow voice, angry voice, sad or happy voice, etc. If movement is included, that can help to support the change of voice. When I taught in reception, I used to sing 'Do Your Ears Hang Low' in a high squeaky voice with tiny movements or in a big, giant voice with huge movements. 'Humpty Dumpty' was recited in an angry voice stomping on the floor, in an excited voice skipping round the room or in a scared voice creeping and tiptoeing. The main objective is to explore sound, both by listening to different sounds and by making different sounds. It is not a 'training programme', but provision of a wealth of opportunities to develop phonemic awareness through play.

Articulation of phonemes

Once children have developed good phonological awareness and have an understanding that print carries meaning, then it is appropriate to introduce linking sounds and letters. It is important that professionals articulate the sounds as purely as possible to provide the best opportunity for children to blend sounds together. To do this there are two main considerations: a) whether or not the sound can be held on to produce a continuous sound and b) whether or not we put our voice to the sound. If a consonant sound cannot be held on (e.g. 'b', 'd', 'g', 'j', 'c/k', 'p', 'q', 't' and 'ch'), then it is important to minimize the 'uh' sound or schwa vowel following the sound. It is virtually impossible not to produce a small 'uh' sound, as these sounds are made by holding and then exploding the air to make the sound, but it can be made slightly rather than with emphasis. The consonant sounds that can be held on (e.g. 'f', 'l', 'm', 'n', 'r', 's', 'v', 'z', 'sh' and 'th') do not need any 'uh' sound at all, and so these sounds should be made by holding the sound for a couple of seconds, for example 'ffff' or 'mmm', not 'fuh' nor 'muh'.

The second consideration is those sounds which include the use of the vocal chords to make the sound (e.g. 'b', 'd', 'g', 'j', 'l', 'm', 'n', 'r', 'v', 'w', 'z', 'th' as in 'thy' and vowels) and those which do not (e.g. 'c/k', 'f', 'h', 'p' 's', 't' 'ch', 'sh' and 'th' as in 'thigh'). For example, if you try and sing the sound 'ffff' it turns into a 'vvvv' sound, which means 'fff' is voiceless and 'vv' is voiced. When you are using these sounds with children, it is important to avoid putting a voice to voiceless sounds so that they are being made as purely as possible.

It is useful if settings work with parents and carers to ensure that all adults know how to articulate the different sounds to avoid confusing the child. The Letter and Sounds pack (PNS/DfES, 2007) comes with a DVD which shows how the sounds should be made. It could be useful to show this to parents and carers to encourage them to articulate the sounds purely so that there is continuity and parity between home and school/nursery. It can take time to feel comfortable with saying the different sounds because we are not used to saying them in isolation; we are used to making a continuous movement from one sound to another within a word. When teaching phonics, particularly synthetic phonics, the 44 phonemes in the English lan-guage (including the different vowel sounds and digraphs) are taught to be articulated separately. These can then be blended for reading or segmented for spelling.

Practical task 3.1

Practise saying all of the different consonant sounds, including digraphs. Are you able to identify the two aspects of sounds: those which can be held on or not and those which are voiced or not? Practise until you feel comfortable and secure with the way the sounds are made.

Reflection for early career professional

- Why is correct articulation of phonemes important?
- How will you ensure other adults working with you pronounce the phonemes in their purest form?

Reflection for leader/manager

- How might you organize a staff development event that would ensure that your staff knew and understood how to articulate the phonemes?
- How would you communicate this to parents and carers?

Phonics schemes

There is a wide variety of commercial phonics schemes that can be used to teach phonics. The Rose Report (DfES, 2006a) strongly recommended fidelity to one phonics programme rather than dipping in and out of a number of different schemes. The main reason for this is the importance of a systematic, structured approach. When I was teaching in the 1980s and 1990s, I taught phonics everyday for approximately 15 minutes each morning. This meets one of the Rose Report's recommendations which states that discrete, daily sessions of phonics should be taught. I did not use any scheme which meant I introduced letters based on a handwriting scheme rather than having knowledge of the most appropriate groupings of letters to be introduced for phonics in a structured way. A scheme provides a clear system which is shared by all those working in the setting. However, when looking for a scheme there is more to it than knowing which GPCs to introduce first and at what pace. A key component is a multi-sensory approach which engages children in movement and games as well as visual and auditory learning. It is also paramount that phonics is taught with enthusiasm and commitment (Wray and Medwell, 2008) and with creativity to ensure the learning is fun and active.

Case study 2

Julie is in charge of the EYFS unit and has been asked to update the phonics scheme. She is considering a range of aspects such as attractiveness of the resources, range of activities suggested, pace of introduction of new phonemes, an easy-to-follow structure, matching books and support for assessment. She decides on one scheme but feels that there are insufficient activities and so decides to supplement these with activities from another scheme. Although she is taking ideas from a second scheme, the structure of the main scheme will be followed to ensure a systematic approach by all staff. Julie's main concern is ensuring that all staff become familiar with the scheme quickly and feel confident in using it. She is also keen that the same vocabulary is used by all staff, which means introducing new terminology, such as phoneme, grapheme, diagraph and GPCs.

Reflection for early career professional

- Have you received any training on how to develop phonological awareness or how to use the phonics scheme? If so, how did this support you? If not, how do you ensure you feel confident in developing children's phonics skills?
- What are the positive aspects of your phonics programme and how could it be improved?

Reflection for leader/manager

- How was the phonics programme in your setting selected?
- How do you ensure all staff know how to use it effectively and share the same terminology?
- Assess the impact the phonics programme has on children's reading and writing. Are there any aspects you feel could be improved or developed?

A phonics session

Daily phonics sessions may well follow a similar pattern. Letters and Sounds (PNS/DfES, 2007: 49) suggests

- Revisit and review previous GPCs learnt
- Teach the new GPC
- Practise the new GPC
- Apply the new GPC by reading or writing a caption with the teacher with the new GPC in a word or words and including high-frequency words

If professionals adopt this teaching sequence, as outlined above, they need to be careful that it does not become boring for the children. The first part can be very quick, but the 'teach' and 'practise' parts need to be practical, active and engaging. The application is commendable, but if children only associate the GPC with the written caption at the end of the session, they may well not apply it in other contexts. Lambirth (2005) is concerned that rigid, strict approaches to the teaching of phonics will result in an over-didactic approach to pedagogy, which will not motivate children to read. This is a legitimate concern because although we may be providing children with the skills to read, if they

Photograph 3.2 Phonics in the classroom (photograph by Emma Jordan)

do not want to read or feel motivated to write then teaching phonics has no purpose.

The suggested teaching sequence is useful, particularly for professionals who lack confidence in the teaching of phonics, but like all schemes and sequences, their effectiveness relies on the strength of the teaching. For phonics teaching to be effective, the practitioner needs a good knowledge of phonics, including how to articulate the phonemes, to understand the developmental sequence, to know how to motivate and engage young children and, perhaps most importantly, to understand the purpose of teaching phonics.

Application

No matter how attractive and systematic a phonics scheme is or how enthusiastically a phonics scheme is taught, if children do not apply their phonics knowledge to reading and writing then it has failed its purpose. Phonics is a means to an end, not an end in itself. I know of schools who give certificates to children when they complete each phase of a phonics scheme. Although this could be viewed as laudable in the sense it praises and encourages, it is also slightly concerning that phonics is being viewed as something separate to reading and writing, rather than one important part of the whole process. I also know of children who are able to blend and segment during phonics sessions but do not apply this skill to words in context in a book or when they want to spell. They are seeing the two processes as totally separate and are therefore not applying the skills learnt in phonics to 'real' reading and writing.

One rather obvious and simple approach is to make the links explicit. Tell the children during phonics sessions that this will help with their reading and writing; highlight any letters or words written or read that have been taught as part of a phonics session; apply children's knowledge of GPC when sharing stories. It is also important to put letters and sounds into a context during phonics sessions so that the children begin to make the links themselves. Being explicit about why the children are learning phonics, rather than keeping it a mystery, will help to reinforce the links to reading and writing.

Providing opportunities for exploring letters and sounds during play enables professionals to assess how much children are able to apply phonics knowledge and skills to their reading and writing. Letters in the water tray, magnetic letters, trays of wet sand for drawing, paper and pencils, paint, chalk outside, word processing and so on allow children to manipulate letters to create words. Role-play areas with writing opportunities such as a baby clinic with appointment books, prescriptions, labels, note pads, charts and so on give children opportunities to write for a purpose. Free access to a wide range of books including comics and catalogues and awareness of environmental print provide children with opportunities to apply their knowledge of letters and sounds to identify letters and words in print. It is important that professionals observe children's play with print to see how much they are applying their phonics knowledge. If it is not apparent that they are, questions should be raised within staff meetings about why this might be the case and what needs to be done to ensure children apply their knowledge when reading and writing.

Case study 3

A Foundation Stage Unit in a Primary school.

Joel was looking at books in the reading corner. He picked up a book called Jack's Day and said 'J for Joel. That says Joel'. He then proceeded to turn the pages and make up his own story.

Ruby was writing a card for her baby sister. She was carefully writing the name Pippa. She sounded out 'p' 'i' 'p' and then put a 'y' on the end. She announced that said 'Pippa' and then wrote 'Love Ruby xxx' with both words spelt correctly.

Emma was writing a shopping list. She wrote 'egggs', 'btr', 'jam', 'shgur', 'bred' and 'milk'.

Reflection for early career professional

- What phonics knowledge is being demonstrated in each of the three examples?
- What other knowledge of words is evident?
- How do you track that children are applying phonics knowledge and skills in their reading and writing?

Reflection for leader/manager

- What systems are in place to see if children are applying their phonic knowledge and skills during child-initiated play?
- How do you monitor application of skills in teacher-led activities?
- What action would you take if application of skills was not evident?

Photograph 3.3 Writing wall (photograph by Emma Jordan)

Most phonics schemes recognize that not all words can be blended by their individual phonemes, and these words have to be learnt using the 'look and say' or 'whole word' approach. Letter and Sounds (PNS/DfES, 2007) refers to these as tricky words. Many high-frequency words do not follow a predictable phonics pattern, such as 'the' and 'said', and these need to be taught alongside the systematic introduction of GPCs. Although some parts of these words could be sounded out, teaching them as a whole word is often more effective.

Transition to Key Stage 1 (5 to 7 years of age)

The Rose Review (DfES, 2006a) states that all children should start learning systematic phonics by the age of five. This means that most children would have started a phonics programme in their reception year. This has clear implications for transition from YR to Y1 to ensure that there is continuity and progression. It is crucial that the staff in the EYFS and KS1 share the same understanding of phonics, and it would seem logical if they used the same programme. In Letters and Sounds (PNS/DfES, 2007), the programme for KS1 moves to a less-regimented introduction of GPCs within weekly time scales to a broader approach focusing on more complex phonic combinations, exploring different graphemes for the same phoneme ('a-e' in ate; 'ai' in rain; 'aigh' in straight; 'ay' in day) and with the emphasis on reading and spelling. Clearly, although the programme has a Y1 and Y2 set of suggested activities and content, it cannot be assumed that all children in Y1 and Y2 will be ready for these. This is why good liaison between the EYFS team and the KS1 team is vital to ensure learning is appropriate and personalized.

Case study 4

The Y1 teacher is looking at the phonics records from the reception year ready to start his planning for the new intake in September. He notices that out of the 27 children, 2 are on Phase 1 of Letters and Sounds, 4 are on Phase 2, 10 are on Phase 3, 8 are on Phase 4 and 3 have started Phase 5. He knows that as he only has one teaching assistant, it will be difficult to organize his phonics sessions in all these separate groups.

Reflection for early career professional

- How might you approach this if this was your class?
- How do you liaise with the staff of younger children and the staff your children will be going to after leaving your class to ensure continuity and progression?

Reflection for leader/manager

- How do your staff organize their children to ensure differentiation is appropriate and learning is personalized?
- Are there strategies you could use to try to ensure there are not so many separate groupings yet still meeting the individual needs of all children?
- How are transitions organized in your setting to ensure they are as smooth as possible? Are there any areas that could be improved?

Conclusion

The EYFS (DCSF, 2008) emphasizes the importance of phonics by making it a specific aspect within Communication, Language and Literacy, and Primary Framework for Literacy and Mathematics (DfES, 2006b) has Strand 5 as the focused phonics strand, which is supposed to be completed by the end of Year 2. The Rose Review (DfES, 2006b) clearly states that phonics is a very important part of early reading and should be taught systematically by the time children are 5 years of age. This focus on phonics could become so emphasized in early years settings that the other crucial aspects of early reading such as a language-rich environment, listening to stories and rhymes, sharing books, talking about stories and using stories in play could become sidelined. Professionals need to know and understand their children to ensure they meet their individual needs. There are compelling arguments to suggest that a child's knowledge of linking sounds and letters to enable them to blend for reading and segment for spelling is a key component of early reading and writing. There is also equally compelling evidence that singing with children, reading with children, sharing books together and fostering a love of story and language is a key component to success in reading and the motivation to read. Phonics is one part of a much bigger process to support children's developing reading and writing skills, and the next two chapters will examine the process in the development of literacy.

References

Boys, R. (2008) 'Communication, language and literacy', in Basford, J. and Hodson, E. (eds) *Teaching Early Years Foundation Stage*. Exeter: Learning Matters, pp. 67–84

DCSF (2008) *Setting the Standards for Learning, Development and Care for Children from Birth to Five; Practice Guidance for the Early Years Foundation Stage*. London: DCSF

DfES (2006a) *Independent Review of the Teaching of Early Reading (The Rose Review)*. London: DfES

DfES (2006b) *Primary Framework for Literacy and Mathematics*. London: DfES

Dombey, H. (1999) 'Towards a balanced approach to phonics teaching'. *Reading*, 33, (2), 52–54

Goouch, K. and Lambirth, A. (2007) *Understanding Phonics and the Teaching of Reading*. Maidenhead: Open University Press, McGraw-Hill Education

Goswami, U. (1995) 'Rhyme in children's early reading', in Beard, R. (ed.) *Rhyme, Reading and Writing*. London: Hodder and Stoughton, pp. 62–79

Hall, N. (1987) *The Emergence of Literacy*. London: Hodder and Stoughton

Johnston, J. and Nahmad-Williams, L. (2009) *Early Childhood Studies*. Harlow: Pearson Education

Johnston, R. and Watson, J. (2007) *Teaching Synthetic Phonics*. Exeter: Learning Matters

Lambirth, A. (2005) *Reflective Reader Primary English*. Exeter: Learning Matters

Lockwood, M. (1996) *Opportunities for English in the Primary School*. Stoke-on-Trent: Trentham Books

Merchant, G. (1999) 'Early reading development', in Marsh, J. and Hallet, E. (eds) *Desirable Literacies*. London: Paul Chapman, pp. 68–84

PNS/DfES (2007) *Letters and Sounds*. London: DfES

Whitehead, M. (1990) *Language and Literacy in the Early Years*. London: Paul Chapman

Whitehead, M. (2009) *Supporting Language and Literacy Development in the Early Years*. Maidenhead: Open University Press, McGraw-Hill Education

Wray, D. and Medwell, J. (2008) *Primary English*. Exeter: Learning Matters

Reading

Chapter Outline

Introduction

The drive to connect with others who make one feel that important sense of belonging and being valued is perhaps one of the most significant factors in a child's language development. In a culture where communication through the *written* word is an imperative and where the ability to read is often associated with general intelligence, carers soon start to introduce their children to the particular patterns of written language. Very often, this will include an introduction to the kinds of book 'behaviour' that are used as indicators of early literacy such as holding the book the right way up, turning the pages, looking at each page in turn, talking about the pictures and reading the text. The early development of reading abilities is often linked with potential academic 'success' and by association with future 'happiness'. Consequently, parents and carers tend to worry more about their child's reading development than they do about any other part of their learning.

The transition from children's experiences of sharing books with their parents or carers to becoming fully independent as a reader is a difficult one to manage. When should children begin the formal business of learning to decode text and draw meaning from the text itself on their own? One of the difficulties here is the idea of a clearly defined starting point at which 'learning to read' begins, a point at which an adult decides that a child should start to learn the skills necessary for successful reading (even if that child is not actually ready to do that).

What is reading?

It is important that we are clear about what we mean by 'reading' to enable us to begin to develop our thinking about these issues. The Rose Review of the teaching of early reading (DfES, 2006) describes early reading development as involving an inter-relationship between two aspects, 'word recognition' and 'language comprehension'. These are presented by Rose as a visual model referred to as the 'Simple View' of early reading development. The first element, 'word recognition', involves two important aspects:

1 When reading words that are unfamiliar, the child will need to recognize the letter shapes (graphemes) and the sounds (phonemes) that each of those represents and then blend together all the constituent phonemes to produce the word.
2 Some key, high-frequency words will be recognized on sight without this blending process being needed. Successfully completing this process is no mean feat, particularly when the complications of the English spelling system are taken into consideration!

The second aspect of reading according to Rose's 'Simple View' is 'language comprehension'. The point here is that being able to decode a word does not in itself enable the reader to understand the message that the author intended in writing the text. There are many ICT applications available to us now, which are able to produce an audible reading of a text, but the machine that decodes and produces the sounds of the words has no real understanding of the meaning of the text. It might be able to identify a sentence which strays from the conventional rules of grammar, but it couldn't recognize a brilliantly crafted sentence and its powerful emotional impact on the reader any more than it could identify a sentence as bland and boring. I could make a very passable attempt to read a passage written in French as the GPCs are similar to those of English and I know enough about the differences in French pronunciation to make it 'sound' right; but I am not a fluent speaker of French and certainly don't have enough experience of written French to be able to actually understand what I am reading. 'Language comprehension' is, at a simple level, the ability of the reader to understand the words that are being read. For example, in the sentence 'The boy jumped over the wall', it is important to know what 'a boy' and 'a wall' is and what 'jumping over' involves to gain a literal, surface understanding of it. However, language comprehension is also about the reader's ability to draw on their own first hand, personal experiences, their general knowledge and their stored bank of responses to other texts, both written and visual, to gain an understanding of a text which goes beyond the literal. Browne (2009, p. 34) uses the three levels of reading comprehension identified by Guppy and Hughes (1999) in her discussion:

1 'Reading the lines – using phonic, graphic, contextual and syntactical strategies to make literal meanings.
2 Reading between the lines – understanding the author's intentions and implied meanings.
3 Reading beyond the lines – reacting to the text, appreciating and valuing the author's meanings, understanding and evaluating the author's craft.'

The successful reader makes connections between their own language comprehension and the language used by the writer to construct a very personal and individual understanding of the sentence. And so, in our example given earlier, the reader might recall a personal experience of jumping a wall to escape from someone or something or they might recognize the 'up to no good' message implied by the sentence from a film or cartoon they have watched. They would combine these responses with a general knowledge that jumping walls is not usually a sensible or safe thing to do depending on how high or stable the wall is to produce their own, individual understanding of the sentence. Smith (2004) suggests that the development of reading comprehension is simply a continuation of the search for meaning that we engage in from birth. Smith (2004: 2) states 'Trying to make sense of any facet of the environment, including print, is a natural activity.'

A successful reader can therefore be described as someone who *does* respond to a text at this deeper level. A successful reader reads intentionally, with a purpose and with the *expectation* that the text will have something 'new' for them to learn or reflect on or that they will gain information that will be of use to them.

Reflection for early career professional

- What are your own attitudes to reading? For example, do you read for pleasure? Do you yourself read with an expectation that you will learn or experience something new?
- How do your own attitudes to reading impact on those of the children you work with?
- What is your internal response when a child asks you to read with them?

Reflection for leader/manager

- How do you ensure that your staff/colleagues have a shared understanding of what reading is?
- How are positive attitudes to reading clearly communicated in the setting's environment? How are these values communicated to the children and their carers?
- How do you share your staff's attitude to reading with parents?

Chapter 3 mapped out the development of word recognition skills, the development of phonological awareness and consequent phonic knowledge, understanding and skills. In this chapter on 'reading', we will consider the development of language comprehension – the ability to understand, interpret, engage with and respond to a range of different texts as 'reading' is described in the National Strategies' Framework for Literacy (DCSF, 2009). There are obvious links with the Language for Communication and Language for Thinking aspects of Communication, Language and Literacy (DCSF, 2008), but here we will look at how those skills relate specifically to the written word. We will also consider very carefully how children's attitudes towards reading and themselves as readers can be nurtured and developed in the EYFS.

Reading from birth to 3 years of age

Even before birth, children are beginning to communicate and learn about the patterns of speech and the turn-taking rhythm of conversation. An expectant mother will respond to their baby's sudden kicks and wriggles by speaking to them and will sometimes then wait for the baby to move again before taking another turn in the 'conversation' themselves. Once a baby is born he will very quickly learn that his cries of hunger, discomfort, boredom or fatigue will elicit a response from his carers – a cuddle, food, movement and comfort. After only 2 or 3 months, babies capture their carers' attention by smiling and, later, laughing, binding them tightly into close relationships where the development of the child's language for communication flourishes. In the context of these positive relationships the children continue to develop their communication repertoire, rapidly building their vocabulary of words, intonations, facial expressions, gestures and body language and learning how to use these in combination to communicate their needs, wants, feelings and ideas in the most effective manner.

This process of building familiarity with and competence in the complex nuances of language for communication also plays a vital underpinning role in the early development of reading. As we have already seen, reading is much more than simply decoding letters to produce the appropriate words – a machine can easily complete that task. Reading in the context of this discussion is crucially the ability to understand the author's intended meaning of the words at a surface, literal level and also to make a range of connections with that message to understand it in a more personal, individual way. If a child has not developed the ability to engage with others' ideas and feelings using oral language, he or she will not be able to engage with an author's ideas and feelings when he reads a text.

This might seem to be an over-complex expectation for under-threes, but many 2-year-olds would recognize and respond to the misdemeanours of a picture book character with the same pantomimed frown, shake of the head and 'Naughty!' that they might have received themselves from their parent or carer. Making these personal connections with the texts that they encounter is an early indicator of reading comprehension although, interestingly, practice in KS1 (QCA, 2009) and beyond would often seem to suggest that reading comprehension is an advanced step in reading development, a more complex, higher-order skill to be developed *after* the decoding skills of phonics and word recognition have been firmly established. It would appear that very young children are indeed able to respond to the texts that they encounter, and the fact that they often have 'favourite' books and rhymes suggests that they are also able to make evaluative judgements.

Once babies are able to hold objects they are often given books that are constructed from thick board, fabric or plastic with 'pages' that present a range of textures, sounds and visual stimuli such as reflective surfaces or bold, highly contrasting patterns. Some board books present a series of simplified images of everyday objects – a cup; a teddy; a biscuit – or photographs of animals or faces; others present an 'untearable' version of a picture book such as Helen Oxenbury and Michael Rosen's classic *We're Going on a Bear Hunt* (Oxenbury and Rosen, 1997) in a size that fits a toddler's hands. A baby's response to these books will often of course be to put them in his or her mouth, and any independent interactions with them are more to do with sensory experiences of touch, taste, vision and hearing than with reading (Mallett, 2003). However, these books will also be used by carers to begin the child's initiation into the

Photograph 4.1 Baby with a book (Photography by L Nahmd-Williams)

patterns of readerly behaviour that are a significant cultural marker in any literate society. This readerly behaviour is partly to do with modelling how to hold a book, which way up it goes or which way the pages turn, and it is also about how we interact with a book, with its images and its text. Shirley Brice Heath's research into the carer/child book interactions of different social groups clearly demonstrated that sharing a book with a child is not a set of fixed, socially and culturally transferable behaviours (Heath, 1982). Some carers will use a book with a child in a way that focuses on 'labelling' the items in the illustrations, asking 'what?' questions of the child, whereas others will explore 'why?' questions, exploring the motivations of characters and making predictions about what they might do next or making links with the child's own experiences. Through these early experiences of reading, shared with their carers, children learn different ways of interacting with books and also develop different expectations of what they will gain from the experience.

Case study

Katie is 11 months old. She has an elder sister who at almost 5 years of age has developed a passion for books and reading, which means that at home Katie sees and is involved in story reading several times a day. Katie is sitting on the living room floor and about 10 picture books are spread out around her. She crawls over some of the books and then sits up on top of one of them. She looks around and then crawls over to another book *Where's My Teddy?* by Alborough (1992). She sits up again and picks up the book. She turns it in her hands until it is the right way up and looks at the front cover. Using both hands she opens the book and looks at the pages where it opens. She turns to another page, points at something in the book and makes a surprised sound. Katie then looks across the room at her mum and holds the book out to her.

At only 24 months, Beth already has a personal library of picture books. A particular favourite is Eric Hill's *Spot's Birthday Party* (Hill, 2003), a lift-the-flap book that she regularly shares with both of her parents. In this story, Spot's party guests play hide-and-seek. The reader 'helps' Spot to find them by lifting the flaps. On each page the repetitive text asks 'Where's Monkey?', 'Where's Hippo?', etc. Beth's parents read the book with her at her request. They allow her to hold the book and turn the pages in her own time, and Beth chooses where to begin reading. As the pages turn, Beth points at the pictures and gives the names of the

⇨

Case study—Cont'd

animals and her parents respond to her comments. They point to the text and read it, encouraging Beth to wait until they have done that before she lifts the flaps. When they reach the page where the monkey is hiding Beth whispers, 'He's hiding! Shhhhhhhhh!', putting her finger to her lips and curling up her shoulders a little to emphasize the need for a careful quietness. When she then lifts the flap Beth is always delighted to find the monkey hiding there. Her parents respond with equal surprise and make comments like 'Oh! There he is! What a brilliant hiding place!'

Reflection for early career professional

- How could the behaviour of these two children be described as 'reading'? What attitudes, skills, knowledge and understanding in relation to reading does each of them demonstrate?
- How do you think Beth's and Katie's parents have influenced their children's reading development?
- Think about your own approach to reading with the children in your setting. What aspects of Beth's parents' approach can and do you emulate? If your approach to reading with children is very different why is that the case? What might you usefully change?

Reflection for leader/manager

- Audit the provision for reading in your setting. Is it organized in such a way as to facilitate closeness in the interactions between children and adults as they share books together? Are there quiet, comfortable areas to sit and a range of quality, age-appropriate books? Can children always find a practitioner who is willing to read with them at any time during the day? How might you further enhance the range of opportunities available for children to engage in quality book-sharing experiences?
- Review the range and quality of the books available in the baby unit of your setting. How do you ensure that the practitioners working with the under-threes know how to effectively share books with babies and toddlers?
- How do you provide parents and carers with the opportunity to talk about their child's favourite books with their key person in the setting? How might you ensure that these favourite books are available in the setting too?

Throughout these early years a language-rich environment is vital as the foundation of reading development. When children under the age of three experience songs, rhymes and stories as part of their daily routines, they will soon develop favourites, and if the adults around them often make links between these and the child's experiences, then they will also begin to do this themselves. For example, the experience of finding and closely observing an earthworm and delighting in the sensation of it wriggling on your hand might be made even more significant if an interested and enthusiastic adult also sings 'There's a worm at the bottom of the garden, and his name is Wiggly Woo!' and encourages the child to join in with making his or her own wiggly movements. Much later, just that song can trigger a whole series of visual, auditory, tactile and kinaesthetic memories for the child, which can help him or her to understand at a much deeper level other references to earthworms in new stories, poems, television programmes or non-fiction texts. Children who experience this kind of language-rich environment are often very successful in their later literacy development, becoming readers who engage with texts at the deeper level of someone who expects to gain something positive from each encounter with them. Weinberger (1996) reviewed several key studies that had identified a link in relation to the home literacy environment and future success with school literacy achievement. Her own research demonstrated that when children entered nursery having regularly shared storybooks and a wide repertoire of nursery rhymes with their parents there was a positive impact on later attainment in reading. In addition, Weigel et al. (2006) studied the impact of parental attitudes towards sharing literacy and language activities with children on later reading development. They demonstrated that when 'facilitative' mothers shared books and engaged in story-related talk and play with their pre-school children there were positive outcomes in relation to children's knowledge about and interest in reading, which persisted longitudinally.

> When parents share books, sing songs, and draw pictures with their children, those parents are providing hours of direct literacy and language experiences for their children. (Weigel et al., 2006: 206)

Key Stage 1 – Reading from 3 to 5 years of age

As children continue to develop as readers, they mature in their expectations of what books and other texts will provide for them. They will continue to have their favourite stories, songs and rhymes and enjoy the feelings of continuity and belonging that their familiar patterns, rhythms and phrases bring. Often, they will jump to chastise and correct any reader who misses out a chunk of one of these stories for speed, insisting that the story be told 'properly'. I consider myself to be a skilled 'performer' of stories, I love to show off with different voices for the characters and a dramatic reading of the text, but on several occasions I have experienced the rejection of a 3-year-old who carefully closes a favourite book after only a couple of pages, slithers down from my knee and firmly asks his mum to read it for him instead! I have failed to follow the familiar and well-loved patterns that that child's principal story-reader has established – perhaps I have not used the right voice or I have turned the pages too quickly or I haven't added the actions that make the book such fun and the experience is thus deemed unsatisfying.

This familiarity with favourite texts can lead to children being able to produce a complete reading of them totally independently, turning the pages in the right places and even sometimes pointing to the text, running a finger under each line as they speak. They may have no understanding of GPCs or even recognize any high-frequency words except for their own name, but they are demonstrating key aspects of the readerly behaviour that underpins successful reading development. For example, they know

- how books 'work' and what their purpose is;
- how to handle books;
- the difference between 'words' and 'pictures';
- that the words that the reader says are 'held' in the written text;
- that the words stay the same each time the book is read; and
- that the voice that you use when you are reading a story is very different from the voice you use when you are talking to someone.

They may also use the pictures as a prompt to help them remember the next section of the text or they may pause in their reading to make comments and ask questions of their listeners. Although this reading is based entirely on memory, it still demonstrates an interaction with the text on a deep, personal level. In addition, if children have developed an understanding of words as whole shapes and they follow these as they 'recite' the story they may also be beginning to build a visual memory of the words.

As children continue in their development as readers they become more and more aware of text in the environment and of purposes of text other than to present stories, poems and rhymes. They are constantly learning how to participate as members of their own cultures, how to use spoken language for different purposes and to meet the needs of different audiences. They start to engage with and respond to the type of language used to recount, to explain, to instruct and to give information, and as they do so they lay down the foundations of an understanding of the written forms of those language genres – their purposes, the 'voice' used in those contexts and the amount and type of detail needed for the listener to understand. For example, the running commentary that adults often give as they engage in everyday tasks – getting dressed, getting ready to go out, putting the child in their buggy or car seat, etc. – begins to establish the sequential structure of explanation, recount and narrative in the child's internal 'language bank'. We know that written language is very different in its nature to spoken language, but in the early stages of language development, as children learn about the different ways that people use language, an understanding of the basic structures of those genres is laid down.

In the home, children may see their carer engaging in reading 'tasks' of many different types:

- reading a newspaper or magazine;
- referring to a map, to road signs or to a set of directions;
- reading a recipe in a magazine;
- reading the prompt boxes on a new console game, the viewing guide on the satellite television system or the menu on a DVD;
- reading signs, labels and packaging in the supermarket;
- reading and writing text messages on his or her mobile phone; and
- reading and writing while internet shopping or using social networking sites.

Many have voiced concerns that the electronic devices that dominate this list are sounding the death knell for literacy (see Crystal, 2001, 2008; Wood et al., 2009). However, the imperatives for real reading comprehension that these 'new' methods of communication bring emphasize the absolute necessity of acquiring those skills. Text messaging, instant messaging and social networking sites on the internet have become key methods of communication,

Photograph 4.2 Reading in the home (© P. Hopkins)

and the ability to use these effectively is closely related to one's ability to gain and maintain a place in a peer group. In addition, access to an infinite breadth of consumer choice and information through the internet has added a new dimension to reading with the particular skills needed to use multimodal texts such as internet shopping websites becoming more and more essential (Flewitt, 2008; Marsh, 2005; Waller, 2008). Certainly, text forms and purposes are rapidly changing and we must be responsive to these, but the ability to decode and understand text is unchangingly important.

Children are also surrounded by print and by written language from the very moment they are born. This environmental print becomes visually familiar to children as they go through their day, both in the home or setting and while they are outside, taking trips to the various places that are part of their particular individual world. This visual familiarity will become useful to children when they embark on the process of learning the links between each letter shape and the sounds it can represent. However, the meaning and significance of this environmental print and the message that it communicates will become obvious to children only if the adults caring for them mediate – using and talking about the text in real contexts.

Case study

At 3 years and 4 months, Jack is able to recognize and name every major super market from their carrier bags. When he is out shopping with his Gran, he readily points out the 'entrance' and 'exit' signs in shops and refers to other signs and labels to help him find particular items. He can link the logo badge with the manufacturer's name for every make of car.

Reflection for early career professional

- What reading skills is Jack exhibiting here?
- How has Jack been able to acquire this knowledge and understanding?
- What role have the adults around him played in supporting this learning?

Reflection for leader/manager

- How do you ensure your setting is rich in functional, meaningful environmental print both indoors and outdoors? How do you make sure the children, parents and practitioners actually have reason to refer to and use it?
- How do your staff/colleagues find out about the children's individual interests and obsessions and how do they then capitalize on those in planning for enhancements to the literacy provision in the setting?

A focus on stories?

Although we have considered the place of non-fiction genres in children's reading development, it is usually stories that tend to dominate any focus on 'reading'. The ability to read and engage with a story does not often have an impact on the everyday lives of most adults. It certainly wouldn't have as much influence on 'success' in adult life as the ability to read and understand a set of instructions; a recount of a particular incident; a discussion of a current issue or a persuasive piece of text. So, why do we spend so much time reading stories to children and encouraging them to develop their reading skills to the point where they can read stories to themselves?

Every culture has storytelling as a key cultural activity.

Telling stories is as basic to human beings as eating. More so, in fact, for while food makes us live, stories are what make our lives worth living. They are what make our condition human. (Kearney, 2002: 3)

We seem naturally to turn every event and encounter in our own lives into oral stories to be shared with others. Our own, personal bank of regularly updated stories are part of our daily interactions with those we meet; they are the social 'glue' that helps us to establish and maintain our relationships with each other at every level; they are the medium that we use to communicate who we are and what we find funny, frightening, interesting or frustrating (Gamble and Yates, 2008).

Children's experiences with narrative begin with the earliest interactions with the significant adults around them as part of the routines of the day. Adults who engage babies in the delights of nursery rhymes and finger plays such as 'Incy Wincy Spider' or 'Humpty Dumpty' are providing them with experiences of simple narratives that will underpin their understanding of that genre as they develop as readers. If those experiences are accompanied by a fixed and often-repeated sequence of actions including tickles, bouncing and rocking, the experience is even more memorable and becomes associated with the feelings of belonging and being loved that are important in the development of positive self-image and motivation as a learner – the young reader will then seek out these kinds of experiences.

Reflection for early career professional

- How wide is your personal repertoire of nursery rhymes, finger plays and action songs to share with children?
- How important do you believe these to be in a child's development?
- When do you sing these with children? Are they confined to 'carpet time' or 'circle time'? What could you learn from a parent's/carer's natural, spontaneous approach to using rhymes and songs throughout the day?

⇨

Reflection for leader/manager

- How do the practitioners working with the under-threes in your setting share songs, rhymes and chants with the children as part of the routines of the day? For example, do they use them at nappy changing, or feeding times or when the children are settling for a sleep.
- How do your staff/colleagues plan to meet the needs of those children who have not had this type of experience in their home setting?

Sharing stories with children

As children develop, adults begin to share stories with them in the form of 'books'. These book-sharing 'events' take many different forms and will alter in their nature and pattern as the children mature. Obviously, children's level of engagement to a story when it is read to them will vary depending on a range of factors:

1 how tired, hungry or content they are;
2 how familiar they are with the adult reading with them;
3 how skilled the adult is at reading with young children;
4 how comfortable the spot chosen for reading is;
5 how interesting the content of the book is to the children;
6 how well written the book is and whether it meets the needs of children at a particular stage of development or
7 how familiar they are with the experience of reading books with an adult.

Practitioners will not necessarily run through this list in a conscious way every time they sit down with a child to read a story, but they are all things that we should be sensitive to – not every child will be quiet and still from page one to the end of the story and nor should we want them to be.

We must also remember that since every reader will bring a very individual set of experiences to a story, their response to it will be unique. It is important that as practitioners we are acutely aware of the possibility of these very individual responses. If we stick blindly to our own individual interpretations and responses to a story that we choose to share with children, we may not be fully receptive to the questions and comments made by the children themselves and as a consequence we may

- miss an opportunity to engage a child in a conversation about something that really interests them;
- fail to help them refine a link they are attempting to make between chunks of knowledge and understanding;
- miss an opportunity to identify interests that might have proved key in engaging children in learning across other areas of learning and development;
- inadvertently give children the message that what they think, their experiences and their interests don't matter to us and that they aren't relevant to 'school' – perhaps setting a negative precedence for their attitude to 'school' (their 'formal' education) and encouraging them to separate 'school' learning from 'real world' learning;
- miss an opportunity to positively influence a child's image of themselves as a 'real' reader – someone who does respond to a text and who reads intentionally with the expectation that there will be something 'new' for them to learn or reflect on.

Successfully reading a story to children does involve a significant amount of 'performance' ability – a good story-reader will use their voice, facial expressions

Photograph 4.3 Children reading (photograph taken by Emma Jordan)

and actions to make the experience captivating and 'significant' – but early years practitioners cannot afford to become 'precious' or 'possessive' about story-reading 'events'. We need to have the flexibility to enable us to respond to the children – they aren't merely an audience, they are active participants – sharing control of the story as it unfolds, shaping it through their responses just as much as the practitioner will shape it through their reading or presentation.

Case study

Jamie is a newly qualified teacher working in the nursery unit of a large children's centre. Many of the children are playing in the outdoor area. Jamie takes a small selection of familiar stories outside and invites the children to sit with him to read some of them. He is joined by five children, four of whom are boys. Most of the children sit very close next to Jamie and one child stands at his shoulder. They choose 'Marvin Wanted MORE!' by Theobald (2006) as their first story. Jamie talks about the front cover of the story, reminding the children about the main characters and then he begins to read. He uses an animated voice to read the text and the children listen while they examine the pictures, but at some pages he stops and makes a comment or asks a question and he also responds to the many comments and questions that the children ask. Some of them are sitting close enough to him to be able to point to the pictures and they do this as they comment. On one page there is an illustration of the surface of the moon; one child points out the craters and Jamie responds to this by posing his own questions and sharing factual information about moons and planets. The children are interested in this conversation and ask further questions, but after a short time one of the children says 'Turn the page!' and Jamie continues with the story.

Reflection for early career professional

- How do you approach story reading with your children? Do you only read stories to the whole group or do you also spend time reading to small groups of children or to individuals? Does story reading only happen in particular places or do you use many different locations within the setting? How do these factors alter the impact of the experience on the children's knowledge, understanding and attitudes with regard to reading?
- How involved are the children when you read stories to them? Jamie responded to the children's comments and questions throughout the story,

⇨

Case study—Cont'd

he skilfully wove them into the experience; do you encourage your children to engage in stories in this way? Do you respond positively to this kind of participation?

- How might you use the children's comments and questions to further support their learning and development?

Reflection for leader/manager

- Consider as a staff how you might develop further links between the setting and the home to ensure that you build on and develop children's experiences of story reading.
- How might you ensure that the practitioners in your staff team share a common understanding of key principles and of what constitutes good practice with regard to sharing stories with children?
- How do you maintain 'high quality' in your stock of children's books?

Using stories as starting points

Very often, we will engage in 'responsive' book reading where we let the children choose the stories that they would like us to read. Usually, in these situations, the practitioner does maintain some control over the children's choices in that they will have carefully selected the books that are available in the setting, but we might also offer to read a book that a child has brought from home. Practitioners need to be skilled in reading an 'unseen' book effectively in these situations, but we should also make regular, carefully planned decisions about how stories or poems can be used as a focus, extending and developing a topic or theme. These themes may spring from the interests expressed by the children and noted in the practitioners' observations or from a local or national event (Football World Cup, Red Nose Day, building work in or near the setting, etc.). In planning to introduce or use a story as a focus in this way, practitioners will need to consider a range of different things:

- Will *these* children enjoy this book? Will *these* children find it interesting?
- Are there any ideas or vocabulary words that the children may not be familiar with? How can I introduce and explain these? When will I do that? During my

reading of the story or before I begin? Will I introduce and explain them through enhancements to the continuous provision, through an adult-led activity or through an experience outside the setting like a walk in the woods?

- What links can I make to other stories that the children are familiar with?
- What other texts – fiction, non-fiction, or ICT-based – could we use alongside this focus story?
- How can I enhance the story-sharing experience here? What props could I use? (Cloaks and hats? Puppets? Small world toys?) How can I use my voice? What voice shall I use for the characters? Where shall I read the story? (In the setting's reading area? Outside? In the wood? On the beach?) How could I prepare the setting? (By making it really dark and giving the children torches? Using background music?) What will the children do? (Get comfy and just listen? Join in with phrases and actions?)
- What details in the pictures might I draw the children's attention to? Could I enlarge some of them or make cutouts of the characters? Could I use the interactive whiteboard for this?
- What questions might I ask to help the children understand the characters, the setting or the plot?

Of course, parents and carers are usually very skilled in sharing books with their children and they would not usually 'plan' a book-reading session in this way. As practitioners we should carefully consider why these experiences are so successful, what they contribute to a child's reading development and what we can learn from parents/carers.

- Parents and carers know their children and their interests very well. They know what makes them laugh, what they are anxious about and what their personality quirks are. They have a head start in choosing stories that their children may make a connection with.
- They share their children's past experiences and as a consequence would be more tuned in to the connections that the child might make with the story and with the characters. They can also help the child to make new connections.
- A parent's agenda is not coloured by a 'curriculum' or a sequence of developmental indicators – their engagement in a reading event is genuinely underpinned by a desire to enjoy the experience with their child. They read the book as the author would intend it – as a 'real' reader.
- A book-sharing experience can be very closely associated with the emotional connection the children have with their parents or key carers. For many children, 'story time' is a time when they are physically close to these significant adults, a time when they either have that adult's undivided attention or only have to share it with a small number of other children.

Conclusion

Nobody would deny that reading is a vitally important skill for every individual in our culture – we all use a level of functional literacy each day to navigate our way through our usual routines, through new experiences and around problems that arise. But one of the key messages of this chapter is that reading isn't just about 'surviving' in a literate society. Reading can bring richly rewarding experiences that can help us to connect with our culture and with those people around us in new and different ways. Reading is about engaging with and responding to texts in individual ways.

Many of the scenarios described here have reflected how parents and carers share books and reading with their children in ways that really connect with their individual interests and experiences. As early years practitioners, we must ensure that we fully respect and learn from this example, building on the excellent foundation for reading that many parents provide and ensuring that every child is able to share that very positive experience.

References

Alborough, J. (1992) *Where's My Teddy?* London: Walker Books

Browne, A. (2009) *Developing Language and Literacy 3–8* (3rd edn). London: Sage

Crystal, D. (2001) *Language and the Internet.* Cambridge: Cambridge University Press

Crystal, D. (2008) *Txtng: The Gr8 Db8.* New York: Oxford University Press

DCSF (2008) *The Early Years Foundation Stage.* London: DCSF

DCSF (2009) *Primary Framework.* Available from: http://nationalstrategies.standards.dcsf.gov.uk/primary/primaryframework (Accessed 1 June 2009)

Flewitt, R. (2008) 'Multimodal literacies', in Marsh, J. and Hallet, E. (eds) *Desirable Literacies: Approaches to Language and Literacy in the Early Years* (2nd edn). London: Sage, pp. 122–139

Gamble, N, and Yates, S. (2008) *Exploring Children's Literature* (2nd edn). London: Sage

Guppy, P. and Hughes, M. (1999) *The Development of Independent Reading.* Buckingham: Open University Press

Heath, S.B. (1982). 'What no bedtime story means: narrative skills at home and school'. *Language in Society,* 11, 49–76

Hill, E. (2003) *Spot's Birthday Party.* London: Puffin

Kearney, R. (2002) *On Stories.* London: Routledge

Mallett, M. (2003) *Early Years Non-Fiction: A Guide to Helping Young Researchers Use and Enjoy Information Texts.* London: Routledge Falmer

Marsh, J. (ed.) (2005) *Popular Culture, New Media and Digital Literacy in Early Childhood.* Abingdon: Routledge

Oxenbury, H. and Rosen, M. (1997) *We're Going on a Bear Hunt* (*Walker Story Board Books*). London: Walker Books

QCA (2009) 'Key stages 1 & 2', in *National Curriculum*. Available from: http://curriculum.qcda.gov.uk/key-stages-1-and-2/index.aspx (Accessed 16 October 2009)

Rose, J. (2006) *Independent Review of the Teaching of Early Reading: Final Report*. London: DfES

Smith, F. (2004) *Understanding Reading: A Psycholinguistic Analysis of Reading and Learning to Read* (6th edn). Hillsdale, NJ: Lawrence Erlbaum Associates

Theobald, J. (2006) *Marvin Wanted MORE!* London: Bloomsbury

Waller, T. (2008) 'ICT and literacy', in Marsh, J. and Hallet, E. (eds) *Desirable Literacies: Approaches to Language and Literacy in the Early Years* (2nd edn). London: Sage, pp. 183–204

Weigel, D. J., Martin, S. S. and Bennett, K. K. (2006) 'Mothers' literacy beliefs: Connections with the home literacy environment and pre-school children's literacy development'. *Journal of Early Childhood Literacy*, 6, (2), 191–211

Weinberger, J. (1996) 'A longitudinal study of children's early literacy experiences at home and later literacy development at home and school.' *Journal of Research in Reading.*19, (1), 14–24

Wood, C., Jackson, E., Plester, B. and Wilde, L. (2009) 'Children's use of mobile phone text messaging and its impact on literacy development in primary school'. *Government and Partners. Research.* Available from: http://partners.becta.org.uk/index.php?section=rh&catcode=_re_rp_02_a&rid=16824 (Accessed 16 October 2009)

Writing

Introduction

One of the key difficulties when it comes to discussing 'writing' in the early years is making a decision about when the random marks that very young children make can confidently be called 'writing'. Parents may become anxious when their child's 'work' folder does not contain anything that resembles 'proper' writing but is packed full of paper covered with scribbles and feel much happier when they can see 'real' letters, even if those are only copied from the practitioner's example.

We must make a clear distinction between the transcriptional aspects of writing – handwriting and spelling – and the compositional aspects which involve the writer in making decisions about what words to use and how to organize them on the page so that they meet the needs of the potential reader and communicate the intended message in a way that is appropriate to its purpose. A child's development towards conventional spelling and the skills that are involved in spelling a word correctly have been covered in Chapter 3 on linking sounds and letters. Handwriting and the process of learning to manipulate a writing tool successfully to produce letter shapes that form the written script will be covered in the next chapter. In this chapter, we will explore how children build their understanding of the purposes of writing, how they develop as successful authors, confidently composing effective labels, captions, stories and other text types, and how we can support them in their learning about what makes a successful piece.

What is writing?

In the previous chapter, we identified comprehension as a key feature of reading. Successful readers must, of course, be able to decode the letters that they see; they must be able to turn the letter shapes into sounds and blend those sounds together to produce the author's intended words. However, that skill is useless if the readers are not then able to understand those words or relate to them in anyway. In the same way, successful writers must be able to perform the reverse operation – separating or segmenting the words that they wish to record into their separate sounds, choosing the appropriate letters to represent those sounds and then making the appropriate marks on the paper or screen. However, if a writer chooses words that make no sense to the reader once he or she has decoded them, then the writing is pointless.

> Writing . . . is a powerful organiser of thinking and reasoning and enables us to communicate meaning in a relatively permanent form to an absent audience across space and time. (Mallet, 2005: 349)

Spelling and handwriting are important in that they ensure that the message gets though to the 'absent audience' with no need for mitigation from the writer. If the message itself is poorly composed, it doesn't matter how good the handwriting is or how perfect the spelling is; it will still be a poorly composed message that will fail to affect the reader in the way that the author intended.

We will consider the vital role that spoken language development plays in successful writing development, but we must also be aware of the differences between written and spoken languages. First, since the purpose of writing is to communicate with an absent audience, writers will not receive immediate feedback from every one of their potential readers in the same way that speakers usually receive it from their listeners. At the beginning of their writing development, children will receive feedback from a parent or carer or from an early years practitioner, but ultimately they will need to learn that a piece of writing has to give all of the information the reader may need to understand the message. Skilled writers must anticipate the questions that their readers may raise and the links they may or may not make. Secondly, writers have the luxury of being able to return to and edit the words and phrases that they use having carefully considered the needs of the reader. Writers can in this way craft and shape the text until they are ready to make it available to their readers, whereas this is not the case when we engage in spoken language – there is often very little thinking time available for us to consider and map out our comments before we have to deliver them.

Writing takes many different forms for different functions. The decisions the writer makes depend on the purpose and the audience for the writing. Some writing is purely functional; this includes genres such as instructions, explanations, labels and captions, recounts and reports. These are usually written to achieve a very specific, fairly predictable result for the readers – they will know exactly what steps to take to achieve a particular outcome when they follow the instructions; they will understand exactly what happened in an event when they read the report; they will gain an appropriate amount of knowledge about a particular topic when they read a non-chronological report. The intention of the writer should be to communicate the message in a way that does not leave it open to re-interpretation. Fiction and poetry have a different purpose again; usually, their intention is to entertain their readers to give them a route into events, actions and emotions that are either completely outside of their own, everyday lives or that reflect reality for them in a new, possibly challenging way. In these types of writing, authors may have a particular reader response in mind when they write and they craft their words carefully to achieve that, but they cannot accurately anticipate what each reader's personal response will be since they cannot know what those readers will each bring to the comprehension process. These types of writing aim to touch emotion, and since emotion is a complex and individual thing, the response of the reader can be anticipated but never truly and accurately be predicted.

For both of these types of writing, there are particular conventions of layout and language structures to follow, which may be socially or culturally constructed. For example, a set of instructions usually gives a clear indication of the overall goal, lists the equipment and materials needed and gives a sequenced list of instructions written in the imperative form. A story would usually introduce the characters and the setting in the opening, build to a dilemma which would then have to be resolved and then conclude by drawing everything together. A story may draw on all sorts of cultural references to evoke the emotional response (fear, pain, sadness, disgust, etc.) that the writer intends. These rules and conventions can, of course, be bent and broken, but the impact of that move will only be effective if the reader is already familiar with the conventions (Mallett, 2003; Riley and Reedy, 2000).

A third type of writing could be called 'personal writing'. This could include diary writing, where the audience is really oneself. Other examples such as letters, e-mails or text messages, which are written to one's personal acquaintances, are very differently loaded. The writers here know the audience, they share past personal experiences and the content of previous conversations, which can be alluded to in subtle ways, and they can use what to others might seem to be obscure references. The audience is known, the text is impacted by that shared understanding and the demands of the writing process are very different.

Writing is about intentionally communicating a message. An effective writer chooses the words they will use, the way that they are ordered and the way they are presented on the page very carefully to ensure that the message is communicated as clearly as possible, to affect the reader in the intended manner.

This discussion may again seem to be far too complex and sophisticated considering that we have the writing development of children from birth to age five as our focus here, but these are the knowledge, understanding and skills that children need to acquire to become successful writers. In addition, it is vitally important that practitioners working with very young children really understand the knowledge, understanding and skills that writing and being a writer involve so that they can effectively support early learning and development.

As soon as children start to communicate, they are beginning to learn about how they can influence others through their use of language. As we have discussed in the previous chapter, they learn to use spoken language to instruct, to explain or to give a recount of a personal experience in a way that engages the listener. As they experience a wider range of texts as readers, they start to learn how the language of those differs from the spoken forms, and in an encouraging environment, where they are presented with real purposes for making their writing effective, they begin to try out these forms for themselves and learn how to be writers.

Writing from birth to 3 years of age

As we have seen, babies begin to learn about communication and interaction even before they are born. The drive to communicate, to make one's feelings, needs and wants known and to interact as part of a community is key in every individual's personal, social and emotional development and forms the foundations for later development as a writer in a literate society.

However, in terms of what children up to the age of three actually 'produce', we have a further issue to consider – at what point could we describe this as 'writing'? As children develop the ability to control their movements, their ability to deliberately produce marks of all kinds emerges. Babies who reach out and grasp for objects – their carer's hair or a toy that is offered to them – are beginning to experience and explore the ways in which they are able to affect their environment and the things in it. Very young children from the age of 4 months or so learn to manipulate the range of materials that they encounter in their everyday lives. For example, they explore how the water in their bath behaves when they try to hold it in their hands or splash and kick it with their feet; when they start to enjoy 'solid' food, they very commonly push it around on the table or highchair tray, squish it in their palms and between their fingers and smear it across their faces.

Initially, children experience these materials in a purely sensory way, with 'What does it feel like?' as their question, but when they are given plenty of opportunity to explore and experience a range of materials that they can manipulate in these ways the question changes to 'What can I make it do?' and at that point they begin to make marks with some purpose rather than as an unintentional by-product of their sensory exploration. They can make marks with their fingers in 'Ooblek' (cornflour and water mixed to a paste that behaves both as a liquid and a solid), in shaving foam and in paint of different consistencies and with additions such as sand or uncooked rice mixed into it, and as they do they will make comparisons between the behaviour of the different media. They may also use different objects as tools, exploring the difference in the marks that these make. In some respects, children repeat this kind of behaviour when they 'arrange' all sorts of different resources in their exploratory play, for example, lining up a set of bricks, emptying a pan cupboard and stacking the pans into a pile. My own elder daughter pulled a bag of potatoes out of a cupboard and arranged them carefully on a tea towel that she had spread on the floor when she was about 2 years old; her satisfaction with having intentionally and thoughtfully produced this 'installation' was written clearly across her face. Children at this stage may well be studying the marks they make in some detail; they may even repeat the same patterns, following their learning schemas, but there is a difference between intentionally making marks and intentionally making marks with the purpose of communicating a message (DCSF, 2008a; Kress, 1997). Children at this stage are beginning to manipulate tools and media to make marks in an intentional way. However, if our definition of writing holds something to do with 'intentionally communicating a message', then this mark making cannot be described as such since there is no message involved. This mark making is a purely physical, sensory experience in the same way that the small child might experience a tactile

Photograph 5.1 Mark making centre (photograph taken by Emma Jordan)

fabric and plastic book by putting it into their mouth or listening to the crackly panels or touching the different textures; these children are doing just what they should, exploring their world through their senses, learning how they fit into it. However, this sensory mark making is the vital precursor to becoming a writer and provides an opportunity for parents, carers and practitioners working with very young children to begin their initiation into the literacy practices of their culture.

A sensitive adult who is tuned in to the development of a child's literacy awareness will often ascribe a meaning to the marks that a child makes suggesting that he or she has written a note to someone or made a list for example. Even though the child had no such intention as he or she was writing, this intervention from the adult can help him or her begin to understand that a seemingly random shape can be given a meaning. Of course, crucially, this kind of intervention will only be effective if the child is immersed in an environment where they see writing for many different purposes being modelled and where the adults explicitly share their intentions as writers with the child. For example, while writing a shopping list or leaving a note for a family member the adults would share the purpose of the writing and speak aloud their thoughts as they decide what to write. This will help them to make a connection between the marks and the fact that they have a purpose although this might not necessarily mean that they understand that there is a message or that the marks relate directly to language. Children at this stage still need to further develop an understanding that the language they speak can be represented word for word in writing.

> ## Reflection for early career professional
>
> - What opportunities do children aged three and under have to explore the behaviour of a range of media that they can make marks in? How do you encourage and support them in asking questions such as 'What does this feel like?' and 'What can I make this do?' How do you support that learning through your use of language?
> - How do you model writing for 'real' purposes for the children you work with? Do you involve them in writing lists, notes and letters that you actually intend to use?
>
> ⇨

- How do you respond to the mark-making activity of under-threes? Does the tool that the children use to make mark affects how you respond to it? For example, are you more likely to respond to marks as 'writing' if the child has used a pen, pencil or thin, black felt-tip pen? How does this affect the child's growing understanding about what writing is?

Reflection for leader/manager

- How do you ensure that your staff/colleagues have a shared understanding of very early writing development and of how to support it?
- How is the setting organized to provide children with opportunities to explore mark making in a range of contexts and using a range of media? Could you develop this in any way?

Key Stage 1 – Writing from 3 to 5 years of age

At some point, often around the age of three, children who have been immersed in a print-rich environment and who have been supported in their writing development by adults who model writerly behaviour will themselves begin to assign a message or meaning to their intentionally made marks. Initially, this may only be in response to the adult's question 'What have you drawn?' or 'What have you written?' and in very general terms – 'It's a dinosaur' – and there may be no correspondence between the meaning the child gives and what they have produced on the paper or even what their thoughts actually were as they made the marks. As they further develop their understanding of how drawing 'works' and of how real objects are represented by two-dimensional shapes and lines, they may begin to explain who or what they have drawn and possibly talk about how the different elements of the picture relate to one another. Equally, as they develop in their understanding of what writing looks like on the page, what writers look like as they write and how writing is used, they will begin to emulate that behaviour, making marks that look more like writing and explaining what it 'says'.

Children's awareness of this distinction between writing and drawing and their ability to apply it to their own marks is closely linked to their under-standing of how text 'works' through their reading development. As they become aware of the difference between written words and pictures in their environment, they are more likely to make that distinction themselves in their own marks, but once again, they will need to have the adults around them supporting their recognition of this difference to enable them to take that next step in their knowledge and understanding about reading and writing. Skilled adults will make explicit to children the significance of the marks they encounter, both as text and as images – helping them to make links between the two-dimensional images of photographs and drawings and the objects they represent and between the text and the words they say and hear. This happens when adults and children read books together, as they chat about the pictures or as the adult points to the text as they read it, but it is also important that adults draw children's attention to the print around them in the environment, reading signs and notices aloud and modelling to the children how these are used. Equally, the adults who write alongside children will be demonstrating to them how to hold the pen, how to move their hand and fingers to produce the letters and that the string of letters and spaces are written from left to right and often from the top of the page to the bottom. They might model the segmenting of the words into sounds and then into letters on the page, and they may draw the children's attention to particular letters, the letters in their name for example. The important thing here is that this is done in a natural, authentic way, not as an artificial, adult-controlled 'learning' opportunity. Usually, children who see the adults who are significant to them actively engaging in the literate world will want to explore, understand and emulate that behaviour. It is also vitally important to make the writers' internal decision-making processes explicit to the child who is sharing the writing experience, with the writer considering out loud the words that could be used, what their impact on the reader might be and how the text might be set out on the page (Browne, 2008; Whitehead, 2004). It is this usually hidden composing process that is the essence of what we are considering here as 'writing'.

During this age phase, children will learn to write their own name, and this often becomes one of the most powerful words in their lexicon, linked as it is to their developing awareness of themselves as an individual and their 'personal identity'. Some children will take their use of this word to the extreme, stamping their ownership on as many things as possible, but it is also very useful when it comes to identifying oneself as the sender in all types of messages, and children love to get a response to the notes that they leave, the cards that they write or even the e-mails that they send (see the case study in the box that follows).

Case study

Jack is 4 years old. His parents have set up an e-mail address for him at home and he regularly e-mails the people on his address list – his mum, his dad, his teenage sister and his grandma. He knows how to select the address that he wants, and since the names of the recipients all begin with different letters he is able to identify them for himself. He knows to start the message with 'Dear . . .' and adds the name using the address box to help him spell it correctly. He ends his messages with 'From Jack'. Sometimes, Jack writes the message in between by himself although at this stage there is no correspondence between the letters that he uses and any message. At other times, his mum or dad will act as scribe and type the message that he wants to send for him. Jack clicks 'send' when the message is ready. He also knows how to open the messages in his inbox and always receives a response to his messages.

Reflection for early career professional

- What knowledge, understanding, skills and attitudes to writing is Jack demonstrating here?
- What impact does the response of the adults involved here have on Jack's confidence and motivation to write?
- How could this type of experience work without the use of ICT?

Reflection for leader/manager

- As a staff team, consider whether it might be possible to enable children to communicate with family members using e-mail in your setting. What might the issues be around internet safety?
- Some of the very common forms of written communication that children will be familiar with outside the setting are not commonly modelled by practitioners, for example text messaging. While it would obviously be inappropriate for practitioners to be communicating with their own friends and family while they are working with the children, could you consider enabling the children to use a setting mobile phone to communicate with their parents or carers? Reflect together as a staff team on the possible implications of this strategy for resourcing, organization and links with parents and carers. How might you address the issue of 'text talk' with its abbreviations and spelling shortcuts?

Photograph 5.2 Children on the computer (Photograph by L Nahmd-Williams)

By about 4 years of age, children who have been supported in their writing development in these kinds of ways will have begun to move on from making 'writing-like' marks to using shapes that resemble conventional letters. They will refine their production of these letter shapes as their handwriting skills develop, and as they also acquire the phonic skill of segmenting along with knowledge of GPCs, their writing will become easier for an 'absent' reader to decode. However, throughout these developmental processes, which actually involve spelling and handwriting, children should also be developing their compositional skills, and it is these that are often neglected by practitioners working with young children when they do not have a secure understanding of what the compositional skills of writing really involve. As Whitehead (2004) points out, there are many studies which have offered an analysis of children's exploration of spelling and handwriting but fewer that look at how children have used writing to communicate a message:

> '. . . it is far easier to describe and evaluate actual marks made on paper than to speculate on the nature and function of meanings and communicative interactions.' (Whitehead, 2004: 181)

As we have seen in the previous chapter, oral language development under-pins the successful development of reading comprehension; a child's develop-ment as an author who is able to clearly communicate a message to an absent audience is also built upon this ability to use spoken language in a range of contexts and for a range of purposes. We have considered some of the differ-ences between spoken and written languages, and through reading and using texts of many different genres, children will become familiar with the particu-lar language structures and organizational features of these. For example, a child of four who is so familiar with a particular written version of a tradi-tional story that they can recite parts of the text may very effectively use phrases from it such as 'once upon a time', 'quick as a flash' or 'without a moment's hesitation' in their own story-telling or narrative play. These phrases are not commonly used in conversational, spoken language, but they are part of the written language of narrative texts. Obviously, this highly developed use of narrative language will only flourish in a child who is immersed in rich language experiences shared with adults who read and tell stories with great skill and enthusiasm. This link between reading and writing applies equally to non-fiction genres. The child who has helped to compose and then use a shop-ping list will understand more thoroughly what the purpose and layout of a list should be. They will then be much more equipped to use that text type effectively both in their role play, where they rehearse the behaviours they have observed, and for their own real purposes.

These are examples of how children between the ages of three and five can begin to develop their abilities to compose effective texts; with the skilled support to which we have referred throughout this discussion, young children are able to compose a message that communicates meaning to an absent reader. It is much more difficult to acquire the transcriptional skills of spelling and handwriting that form a barrier to children's success in producing a piece of writing that records that message permanently, but there is no reason why their development as authors should be held back until they have been able to build those skills. Here again, the role of the adults who support children's learning and development is vital. When adults act as a scribe for children, they release them from the physical and mental demands of spelling and handwriting into the creative business of deciding what to write. This role, however, should extend beyond simply transcribing what children say, as this context is a perfect opportunity for adults to engage them in the kind of sustained shared thinking that is identified by the EPEY project as a feature of high-quality pedagogy in the early years (Siraj-Blatchford et al., 2002). Using this approach, adults and children can work together to find the best way to express the children's ideas, and adults are able to clearly model the decision-making process, including discarding ideas that at first may seem useful, that is the skill of the writer.

Oral language experiences and the writing process

The vital role of rich language experiences in supporting children's writing has been discussed earlier, but the nature of these experiences warrants further consideration. What do these experiences look like in practice? How can we effectively resource them in early years settings? What is the practitioner's role?

One of the key factors in engaging children in successful writing is providing them with something to actually write about. All writers need real, meaningful purposes for writing that truly capture their interest and provide motivation, but they also need to have plenty of opportunities to explore and develop their ideas, their knowledge and their understanding and to refine the language around those experiences before they start to write. Within the play-based EYFS (DCSF, 2008b), children are provided with opportunities to pursue their own interests and to encounter new ideas, experiences and phenomena across all areas of learning and development. When practitioners are skilled in using sustained shared thinking to help children extend and refine their ideas, they also provide the opportunity for them to orally rehearse the language that, for example,

- describes or offers an explanation for the phenomenon they have observed;
- provides instructions to enable another to follow a procedure they have explored;
- narrates a story they have developed; or
- recounts an experience they have had.

The amount of responsibility the children take for actually transcribing the language themselves then depends of course on their spelling and handwriting development and also on the length of the text. They may, by the end of the EYFS, be able to complete the process independently, but equally, some children will need the practitioner to do this and others will be able to do some of the transcribing with the practitioner carefully timing when they step in to take over. The important thing here is that the message that the child has composed is recorded and that it is then 'published' – made available to a 'real' audience. As a justification for this approach to children's writing, balancing the negative pressure of transcription against the nurturing of the composition process, we need to only think about motivation. As we have seen, the transcriptional skills involved in actually producing a piece of text are much more demanding and difficult to acquire than the language-based compositional skills. If we insist that children record everything themselves, there are several potential consequences for their writing development:

- A large part of what they have composed will be lost as they may not have the stamina to enable them to transcribe the whole piece and the mental and physical demands of spelling and handwriting may cause them to forget or confuse their ideas.
- They may lose enthusiasm for the composing process itself, since if they generate lots of language they are then dropped into an over-challenging, time-consuming and tedious task.
- They may fall back onto familiar, formulaic responses – those that they know they can record quickly and easily.

It is, of course, important that children develop their spelling and handwriting skills, but not at the expense of their continued development as authors. Practitioners should find ways of supporting development of these aspects of literacy that keep them separate from composition until they are sufficiently developed for them to have no negative impact on the child's ability to independently record what they have composed.

One example of how oral language experiences can underpin writing development is through children's 'storying'. Children create often quite sophisticated narratives during imaginative play of all types, for example, in their role playing or in play with small world resources. This play can be solitary, but is often experienced by children playing together in pairs or small groups. During this type of play, children define the characters and their relationships with each other; they create and develop the setting for the narrative, thinking about how different features of it might affect both the characters and the development of the plot, and they make decisions about the dilemmas the characters might face and how those might be resolved. Children working together will make the narrative very explicit by providing a running commentary, which may sometimes switch to become a negotiation between the participants of the 'I know, he could climb up this cliff and then hang-glide away to escape!' sort. Children playing on their own sometimes provide an audible running narrative, including dialogue, but they may also keep the language internal. In this case, the observer can only infer what the narrative is from watching the action of the figures. It would also appear that there are at least two approaches to small world play. Some children like to 'animate' the figures during their narrative play, making them climb up 'cliffs' and stop for a chat with another character; others follow a 'scene-setting' approach, placing props and characters in place in what becomes a fixed tableaux. However, these children will also be playing out a narrative internally, which will reflect the action that emerges from the scene they have set up. In short, through this type of play, children can clearly demonstrate their understanding of the narrative genre and their ability to engage with it (Rich, 2002; Whitehead, 2004). As the case study that follows demonstrates, the role of practitioners in supporting this type of language experience includes providing the children with access to a wide range of resources, which they can use to enhance their narrative, but these must be available to children at all times and they must also know what is available to enable them to make informed choices about what they use. Any intervention that a practitioner might make into this kind of play would need to be very carefully timed so as not to disturb the narrative, but it might be useful as a way of extending and developing the narrative so that it can be recorded and possibly turned into a text that can be read. Alternatively, the practitioner could take photos as the narrative develops and these can be used later to reconstruct the story with the child and turn it into a written, illustrated narrative.

Case study

During the first half hour of the morning session in the nursery unit of a large children's centre, many of the children were observed engaging in storying behaviour. Some of the narratives were made explicit as the children gave a running commentary, but others could only be inferred from the children's actions:

⇨

- A girl was walking round the setting with a small baby doll wrapped up in a blanket. As she passed the observer, she said, 'She's going to sleep'.
- Two boys were sharing a large format 'dictionary', on each page of which there were detailed, labelled illustrations to match a theme such as 'At the zoo'. The boy who was holding the book was sitting on a large armchair while the other boy was sitting on the arm of the chair, looking over his friend's shoulder. When the boys turned to the page headed 'The Fairground', the boy holding the book pointed to the part of the picture, which showed two children on a rollercoaster, and said, 'That's you and that's me.' The second boy said, 'Pretend we're on it!' and he slid down from the arm of the chair to sit next to his friend. The two boys then role-played riding a rollercoaster, adding appropriate exclamations as they chugged up to the top of a climb and then shot down the dip.
- A boy and a girl were playing with the small wooden train track on a low table at the edge of the room. The boy said, 'Whoooooo!' as he ran the train along the track and through the tunnels. As he passed the girl, he said, 'This is the train . . .' She did not respond, but continued to push her train along the track much more slowly than the boy. He then said, 'Get the other carriage . . .', fixed a further carriage to his train and then said, 'It's gonna be long.' The girl watched as the boy altered the order of his carriages and then went to collect some more.
- A boy was playing with a small world monkey, jumping it from one surface to another. He did not say anything, but was smiling as he did this. Another boy was playing with a giraffe of about the same size. He made the giraffe 'jump' on the monkey. The child with the monkey squealed happily and ran away. The children giggled as they then played a game together where the monkey and the giraffe chased each other round the low furniture unit in the middle of the room. The child with the giraffe left, and the child with the monkey called, 'Ner, ner, ne, ner, ner!', after him, bouncing the monkey back and forth as he did. The first child then continued moving around the area, jumping the monkey on the different surfaces again and turning it over and over so that it cartwheeled along some of them.
- One child walked through the area with two small world toys – a 'Buzz Lightyear' action figure and a small piano keyboard. As he walked, he made the figure 'play' the keyboard and he was singing, 'Pia-pia-piano, piano, piano . . .'

⇨

Case study—Cont'd

Reflection for early career professional

- Can you identify the narratives that are embedded in the play of these children?
- How might you help the children to extend their play in each of these contexts? Is intervention always appropriate?
- How has the organization and resourcing of the setting influenced the children's behaviour?

Reflection for leader/manager

- How does your setting resource this kind of storying play? Audit the small world toys and role-play costumes and props that are available to the children and consider the 'play potential' that they provide. How do you ensure that the children have continuous and full access to all of the resources so that they are able to seek out what they need to support their developing narratives?
- Explore with your staff team how they feel about the children accessing all of the materials and equipment all of the time. What are the implications for organization of the resources?

Conclusion

A successful writer is able to use words skilfully to lead his or her reader in a particular direction – to feel a particular emotion, to complete a task and to understand a new idea, for example. Even the tiniest baby is able to use communication to elicit a particular response in the parent or carer, and it is possible to see this as the first step in writing development, which we have explored here.

We must be careful to think of 'writing' as 'composition', and this chapter has described the many different ways that children can be involved in the careful crafting of language that composition involves across a range of genre. The role of early years practitioners is key here in that they

- provide the model of writerly behaviour that children will strive to emulate;
- scaffold the oral language experiences that are the starting point of any piece of writing;
- provide a range of resources across all areas of provision and a supportive, language-rich environment;
- provide meaningful purposes for writing and ensure that children receive the feedback they need to maintain their confidence and motivation; and
- skilfully intervene in children's writing experiences to scribe when necessary to maintain the flow of their ideas and to help them develop these ideas further.

With this kind of support, children in the early years are able to produce highly effective, purposeful writing and will develop a positive image of themselves as writers.

References

Browne, A. (2008) 'Developing writing in the early years', in Marsh, J. and Hallet, E. (eds) *Desirable Literacies: Approaches to Language and Literacy in the Early Years* (2nd edn). London: Sage. pp 103–21

DCSF (2008a) *Mark Making Matters: Young Children Making Meaning in All Areas of Learning and Development.* London: DCSF

DCSF (2008b) *The Early Years Foundation Stage.* London: DCSF

Kress, G. (1997) *Before Writing: Rethinking the Paths to Literacy.* London: Routledge

Mallett, M. (2003) *Early Years Non-Fiction: A Guide to Helping Young Researchers Use and Enjoy Information Texts.* London: Routledge Falmer

Rich, D. (2002) *More Than Words: Children Developing Communication, Language and Literacy.* London: The British Association for Early Childhood Education

Riley, J. and Reedy, D. (2000) *Developing Writing for Different Purposes: Teaching about Genre in the Early Years.* London: Paul Chapman

Siraj-Blatchford, I., Sylva, K., Muttock, S., Gilden, R. and Bell, D. (2002) *Researching Effective Pedagogy in the Early Years.* London: DfES

Whitehead, M. R. (2004) *Language and Literacy in the Early Years* (3rd edn). London: Sage

Handwriting

Introduction

At the end of my first term at high school, my English teacher added a comment to my report, which would have consequences for many Sunday afternoons to come. After several positive comments about my general achievement, she added, 'However, her handwriting is appalling'. My father immediately saw this as a challenge. As a talented amateur artist with an eye for graphic design, he had developed a striking and individual handwriting style and was determined that my handwriting would not be 'appalling'. And so, for many Sunday afternoons after that, I was to be found sitting at the dining table, often in tears, practising my handwriting. My dad wouldn't usually have been so authoritarian, but he was very aware that 'appalling' handwriting at a time when job applications were handwritten might well consign my letters of application to the reject pile, no matter how well phrased they were.

Does handwriting style matter so much now that the majority of our formal written correspondence is word-processed and presented electronically? One of the key messages in the previous chapter on writing is that the message is the important factor in any piece of writing, the words that are used and their impact on the reader. If we only use handwriting to communicate with ourselves, drafting out a letter or making notes in a meeting for example, or very informally with close friends, does it matter if it isn't 'beautiful'?

Despite my experiences aged 11 years, I love to write by hand. I love the feel of the flowing movement of my hand and fingers and the pen or pencil on the paper; I love to write on new, smooth paper with a good fountain pen and I did eventually, over about 15 years, develop a personal handwriting style that often receives positive comments (and I always think about that English teacher's comment when it does).

What I have been describing here is not just the legibility of an individual's handwriting; the other facet of the 'appearance' factor is about making handwriting look beautiful. Before the invention of the printing press, the ability to produce script that was a thing of beauty in itself was highly valued, and indeed, calligraphy is recognized now as an art form. I have also mentioned the physical pleasure that I have in producing handwriting, a similar pleasure that a chef might have in using good knives or a joiner in working with real oak. This is handwriting as a craft, producing something of aesthetic value and providing the craftsperson with a positive experience. But handwriting isn't just about presentation and developing handwriting style isn't just about aesthetics. Handwriting is also a functional thing – the means of permanently recording the message composed by the author. Particularly now, when writing by hand is usually either for oneself or for a highly pressurised purpose such as communicating one's knowledge and understanding to a GCSE examiner, the speed and fluency of our handwriting are the important factors, and these are impacted by several other factors such as posture, pen grip, position of paper and letter formation.

So, we should consider

- handwriting as an aesthetic product in itself – an art form or craft;
- the potential pleasure for the writer in the process of producing handwriting and
- handwriting as a means of making a record of the writer's decisions about how to communicate their message to an audience.

Reflection for early career professional

- What do you recall of how you were taught your handwriting skills? What made it a positive (or negative) experience?
- What are your feelings about your own handwriting style and about writing by hand in general?
- Consider the contexts in which you use handwriting. How well does your own handwriting style meet the needs of each context? Think about legibility, fluency and speed.

Reflection for leader/manager

- How do you ensure that your staff/colleagues have a shared understanding of the purposes of handwriting and the issues around the teaching, learning and assessment of it?
- How are positive models of handwritten text and of handwriting as a skill communicated to the children and their carers?

Handwriting from birth to 3 years of age

Before we can even start to think about focusing on the fine motor control needed to hold and manipulate a writing tool to the extent needed for even the most basic intentional marks – vertical and horizontal lines, clockwise and anti-clockwise circles, arches and loops in the case of handwritten text – we must ensure that we have provided the support needed for children to develop their gross motor skills. Muscle tone and strength in the whole body are vital. The large muscle groups in the back, abdomen, shoulders, upper arms, neck and legs provide support for hand, wrist and finger movements; maintain the head position that the writer needs to 'watch' what they are writing and maintain balance and good posture.

Motor development does not only begin at birth of course. A mother may begin to feel the fluttering movements of her developing baby from the eighth week of her pregnancy and later on these become distinct rolling and tumbling movements as the baby changes position and kicking and thrusting movements from arms and legs. This physical development continues following birth as babies seek out and respond to stimulation from their environment. The range of reflex movements which a newborn baby will display in response to particular stimuli, such as the grasping and rooting reflexes, will be accompanied by spontaneous movements with no apparent stimulus. These often appear to be movements for movement's sake with the child absorbed in vigorous kicking, waving and rocking actions along with slow arm and leg flexes following feeds and movement of the fingers and toes. During the first 12 months, babies will gradually develop increasing stability, enabling them to maintain an upright posture as they achieve the 'motor milestones' of lifting and holding the head upright, sitting, standing and eventually taking the first unsupported steps. These changes can only happen with the gradual development of strength in the muscle groups of the back, abdomen, shoulders and neck, and the level of stability that is achieved is vital as it is involved to some degree in all voluntary movement.

> . . . the ability to achieve postural control of the body and move it voluntarily to a desired position underlies all motor behaviour. (Doherty and Bailey, 2003: 29)

Babies grow very quickly and this, along with their drive to overcome the forces of gravity and achieve an upright posture, has an impact on motor development. The gross motor skills lead this development. Cephalocaudal development describes the progress of changes occurring from the head towards the feet as the child matures. Very young children appear to be 'all head' with the head actually making up 20 per cent of the total body length. This proportion will have altered by the time the individual reaches adulthood when the head will account for 12 per cent of the total body length. The impact of this developmental process is that the child will develop the ability to coordinate and control the upper body before the legs and feet – achieving shoulder control before control of the lower back and pelvis. In addition, proximodistal development, occurring from the centre of the body to its periphery, means that control of the shoulders must be well underway before that of the hands, wrists and fingers can become a priority [for more information on physical development, see Cooper and Doherty (2010) in this book series].

This isn't to say that very young children do not have any ability to use their hands and fingers. By 8 months, a baby will usually be able to operate a functional pincer grip, demonstrating very high levels of concentration as he or she tries to pick up small objects such as a pea from the high chair tray. In fact, meal or snack times are a perfect opportunity for parents and practitioners to provide supervised opportunities for children to build their fine motor skill proficiency as foods of different textures can safely be offered in relatively small pieces cut into a range of shapes. Picking these up and moving them to the mouth (or throwing them on the floor) involves a range of motor skills. By 16 months, the ability to seize, grasp and manipulate objects using both hands will be coordinated and fairly proficient, but at 24 months, the use of tools such as scissors for example or the ability to 'colour in' a picture accurately will still need further practice.

Between 12 and 36 months, the basic gross motor skills are practised and further developed so that, for example, balance when walking improves to a point where the child can start to run although the ability to start and stop may not become efficient until later. New movements such as climbing are also added to the repertoire although initially this will take the form of 'marked time' climbing where the following foot is brought up to meet the first, leading foot rather than passing it to take an additional step. These gross motor movements are absolutely vital in laying the foundations for the fine motor skills involved in manipulating the tools used for handwriting or other forms of text presentation; without these as a foundation, the ability to control wrists, hands and fingers cannot develop. In addition, it is while using these big movements to propel themselves through and explore their environment that young children begin to learn about how their bodies work, about movement in different directions, making different shapes and at different levels, and about pushing, pulling, circling and moving over and under. With skilled support and intervention from the practitioners working with them, children will also begin to develop the language used to describe movement, lines of direction and shapes, language that will be instrumental in their readiness to later develop the very specific movements of letter formation.

Often, the first marks that children produce are the random lines and patterns that they make with their hands and fingers in their food. Children who are given the opportunity to push their fingers through yoghurt on their high chair tray are not simply engaging in a sensory experience, exploring the texture and behaviour of the yoghurt as they squish it between their fingers; they are also making their first foray into the essentially human practice of making marks. Initially, these marks are a purely random product of exploratory play, but soon the child will notice the patterns and lines they have produced and will begin to produce them in a more purposeful way. Children will also begin to use the foods they can hold as mark-making tools, pushing them through other mashed or pureed foods. Offering a spoon for the child to hold presents further opportunities for practice of tool manipulation, and although the use of a spoon to transfer food to the mouth is the 'usual' goal, a spoon can also be used to make marks in food. Practitioners can provide children with larger surfaces and other media to explore using their hands and fingers in this way, as described in Chapter 5 – Ooblek, custard, soap flakes, shaving foam, etc. – and they may also add 'tools', such as spoons, fat paint brushes, sponges or small blocks of different shapes, for making marks in these media. Through this type of activity, children are developing an awareness of themselves as a maker of marks while also continuing to develop both the gross and fine motor skills needed for purposeful mark making.

Once children recognize their ability to make marks, they often take every opportunity to do so, particularly when offered access to other mark-making

Photograph 6.1 Young child mark making (Photograph by L Nahmd-Williams)

tools such as pens, pencils, crayons, felt-tip pens, chalks, paint brushes used with paint or plain water, etc. They should also be offered opportunities to make marks on a range of different surfaces – different weights and textures of paper; dry-wipe surfaces; magnetic 'doodle' boards; concrete paving slabs and brick outside. Provision of these kinds of resources gives the child the opportunity to explore and begin to refine the fine motor skills needed to manipulate mark-making tools as they experience and respond to the different textural qualities of both tools and surfaces. Very young children will hold these tools in a palmer grip, the resulting line being the 'visible trace' of a whole arm movement (Sassoon, 1990). With regular further play and opportunities to experience a range of mark-making tools, this will gradually develop into a pincer grip which enables the child to use the wrist and finger movements needed to produce the more controlled marks that written script requires. It is at this point, when children are first aware of their ability to literally 'make their mark', that marks made with any manner of media, including a carelessly abandoned lipstick or eyeliner, may appear on walls, floors, picture books and cupboard doors in the home.

Case study

Katie is 3 years old. She enjoys any activity that presents her with the opportunity to explore textures and tactile experiences. As a toddler, she would regularly rub handfuls of yoghurt into her face and loves to play outside in the pouring rain, splashing in puddles and getting wet. She has opportunities to mark-make at home and her parents ensure that she has access to coloured pencils, crayons, chalks and felt-tip markers and paper of different colours and weights. She has been encouraged to chalk on the path outside in the garden and to 'paint' with water and big brushes on the exterior walls and surfaces, and her mother provides large pieces of paper for her to paint on outside although paint usually ends up all over Katie's hands and face. On one occasion, Katie had walked up and down the hallway at home running a crayon along the textured wallpaper in long lines several times before she was noticed and it could be explained that this was not acceptable. Her mother suggested that Katie probably enjoyed the bumpiness of the paper under the crayon.

⇨

Reflection for early career professional

- How could you ensure that you have this kind of rich information about every child you work with?
- How do you ensure that children in your setting are experiencing a wide range of opportunities for exploring mark making and developing both gross and fine motor skills?
- How might you respond to Katie's individual learning style and interests in a nursery setting?

Reflection for leader/manager

- Audit the range of opportunities for development of gross motor skills available to the under threes in your setting. How do you provide for the complete range of 'big' movements mentioned earlier – running, climbing, swinging, rolling, crawling, etc.
- How do you ensure that there is a shared understanding between the practitioners in your setting of the role that physical play using whole body movement, 'messy' play and activities using malleable materials have in children's handwriting development?
- Working with the whole practitioner team, carry out an audit of the ways that language is used to support and develop children's physical play.

Key Stage 1 – Handwriting from 3 to 5 years of age

From 3 years onwards, children continue to develop their physical skills in line with their growth and development. Bone density increases supporting the child's ability to manipulate their body in increasingly complex ways. As children continue to push themselves physically, running, jumping, climbing and swinging, they begin to

> . . . understand the relationships between the two halves of their bodies . . . they learn where to put their hands or feet and move their bodies in ways they need to. They learn about movement by moving. (Rich, 2002: 14)

This increased awareness of their own bodies and of their physical capabilities and boundaries has an important role in the development of mark-making abilities. To further develop children's skill in moving in these ways, they should be provided with opportunities to climb using ladders, ropes and climbing frames and to play with resources such as hoops, ribbons and large pieces of floaty fabric, which will encourage them to make big, sweeping movements that use their shoulders and core abdominal muscles.

It is also important to consider the role that perceptual motor development plays in children's readiness for handwriting. There are several aspects related to visual perception, for example, that will have an impact:

- Visual acuity – the ability to recognize detail does not normally reach adult levels until the age of 5;
- Spacial orientation – by the age of 4 most children will know the basic 'dualisms' of position: over/under, high/low, etc., and
- Depth perception – the ability to judge how far away an object is will not be fully developed until the age of 12 years.

These are developmental factors that cannot be taught, and so once again, the role of the practitioner is to provide the kinds of physical tasks involving perceptual, gross and fine motor skills that will give children the opportunity to practise and thoroughly establish the skills. These activities will include

- running, climbing, rolling and sliding;
- riding pedal toys;
- walking on stilts and low balancing apparatus;
- rolling, trapping, throwing and catching balls of different sizes and materials or beanbags;
- sharing picture books and discussing the details in the illustrations;
- enjoying finger plays, action rhymes and dancing activities;
- shaping dough and clay and other malleable materials using hands and tools;
- folding, tearing and scrunching paper;
- cutting paper using scissors, either randomly or following lines and
- play with small world and construction kits.

These are all activities that are familiar to early years practitioners as part of the continuous provision in quality settings. The role of practitioners in supporting children's engagement with these tasks is key in that the language they use to instruct children in the specific skills needed, for example, when using scissors, and in sustained shared thinking (see Chapter 2) not only helps children to reflect on and further develop the physical skills but also lays down some of the language that is necessary for describing the movements made when letters are formed (Siraj-Blatchford et al., 2002).

During this age phase, children's mark making also develops to include increasingly 'letter-like' forms, which they see as separate from their 'drawings'. Children bring a culturally situated understanding of the purposes of text from their home experiences, and in an early years setting that is rich in functional environmental print with practitioners who skilfully share books and writing experiences, children become very aware of the visual features of text and the distinction between text and picture. This awareness appears alongside a developing understanding of the exciting potential of marks for symbolizing something else – remember that the child who discovers the power of 'making a mark' will often do so at every opportunity. Between the ages of 3 and 5, children will begin to assign some meaning to the marks they have made. Initially, these may not appear to have any apparent connection to the object, idea, event or words that they have represented, but they have much to learn about the culturally specific ways of symbolizing these things that we use (DCSF, 2008a; Kress, 1997).

As they begin to master the physical skill of manipulating a writing tool using fine motor movements of the wrist and fingers, children who are immersed in a print-rich environment will also begin to try to emulate the visual features of the script type they are most familiar with and the movement behaviours of those they observe writing. This may manifest in a child's mark making as horizontal lines of zigzag, produced at the same speed as an adult writer might produce a piece of text. As they become more aware, they may begin to produce marks, which use separate letter-like forms with circles, loops and vertical lines. Producing these helps to build strength in wrists and fingers for pen grip and letter formation. The first word that most children will write is their own name – this is, of course, a word of great power and significance to any individual. It is a word used to identify possession and to claim independence – it says, 'This belongs to me', 'I made this' and 'I am'. The form of the letters that children use as they work to master the skill of writing their name will depend entirely on the visual model they are most familiar with. If their parent or carer has written their name in their wellies and inside their coat, on their lunch box and on their pictures, bedroom doors, toy boxes and so on using upper case, capital letters, those will be the shapes that children will begin to attempt to reproduce. In addition, these are the letters that are most common in environmental print – road signs, newspaper headlines, labels on cereal boxes, etc. – they are often the shapes that children will be most familiar with.

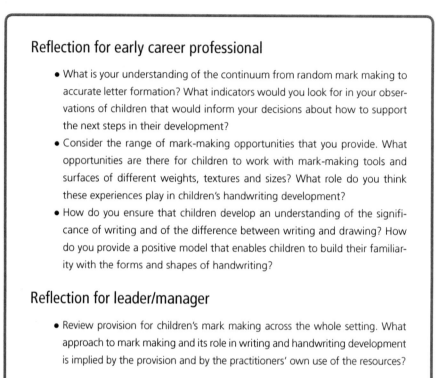

Reflection for early career professional

- What is your understanding of the continuum from random mark making to accurate letter formation? What indicators would you look for in your observations of children that would inform your decisions about how to support the next steps in their development?
- Consider the range of mark-making opportunities that you provide. What opportunities are there for children to work with mark-making tools and surfaces of different weights, textures and sizes? What role do you think these experiences play in children's handwriting development?
- How do you ensure that children develop an understanding of the significance of writing and of the difference between writing and drawing? How do you provide a positive model that enables children to build their familiarity with the forms and shapes of handwriting?

Reflection for leader/manager

- Review provision for children's mark making across the whole setting. What approach to mark making and its role in writing and handwriting development is implied by the provision and by the practitioners' own use of the resources?

Photograph 6.2 Marking making in the sand (photograph taken by Emma Jordan)

Teaching handwriting

Rosemary Sassoon (Sassoon, 1990) is still recognized as one of the key voices in the discussion on the teaching of handwriting. She asserts that children should be supported in developing an individual handwriting style rather than one which follows a strict set of rules, such as when the writer should lift the pen from the paper, and emphasizes the vital importance of correct letter formation, which can then be accelerated through practice to achieve fluency and speed in writing. These two characteristics are clearly associated with a joined, cursive style rather than with a script of separate, printed letters of the 'ball and stick' type.

> We should be trying to train communicators who write legibly, but in a way suited to their own hands and personality, not forgers who can slavishly imitate an impersonal style. (Sassoon, 1990: 6)

Handwriting is 'the visible trace of a hand movement' (Sassoon, 1990: 7), and since we each use our bodies and move in individual ways, that movement will be reflected in our handwriting. Good posture and positioning of the paper are also important, since any position that causes physical stress on the body will not only become painful for the writer, and potentially produce negative feelings about writing as a task, but will also transfer to the handwriting itself.

Since a printed script of straight letters that all 'finish' on the line produces a 'stop' in the movement of the writer's hand, Sassoon recommends adding exit strokes to individual letters as part of the whole letter formation pattern so that they naturally lead into the next letter, building that all important fluency and flow. Some handwriting schemes also add entry strokes to individual letters, but Sassoon's argument is that the exit strokes are sufficient to train the hand to move fluently into the next letter and that with increased practice, which firmly establishes these letter formation patterns, the writers will 'naturally' develop their own individualized cursive script. The majority of mature adult writers have developed their own style with individualized approaches to joins and common letter groupings, and this is not usually criticized as long as the resulting script is legible and the joins do not present the writer with difficulties when speed is required. It could be suggested that insisting on entry strokes, which always start on the line, adds an increased demand on very young writers learning letter formation, which could further delay their progress both with the development of handwriting and as confident writers.

Activity

1 Writing quickly and using your normal, personal handwriting style, copy out this sentence.
2 Look carefully at your writing. Do you join every letter in a whole word or can you see where you have lifted the pen in the middle of some?
3 Write that first sentence again, and this time, try to be more aware of where you lift the pen. Do you cross 't's and dot 'i's when the whole word is complete or as you form them? Do the breaks or pen lifts in some words slow you down or help you to maintain speed and flow?
4 Consider carefully how you link letters and how you make the joins. For example, in the word 'handwriting', do you lead out of the first 'n' and into the starting point of 'd' using a clockwise movement that then reverses to form the anti-clockwise loop of 'd'? This is how most children are taught to join these letters, but, for example, I actually leave 'n' with an anti-clockwise movement, which I continue to form the loop of 'd'.
5 The word 'and' is one that we write very regularly. Have you formed every letter in 'and' completely? Very often, we develop individual ways of writing the high-frequency words to add speed – you might have 'flattened' the 'n' in 'and' so that it is simply a wiggle between clear 'a' and 'd' shapes.
6 Is there any aspect of your personal handwriting style that is actually inefficient? Are there any 'unconventional' letter formation habits that actually slow you down?

Reflection for early career professional

- Having briefly considered your own handwriting style, and in particular the ways that you have developed your own individual approach to joins and breaks within words, what do you consider to be the key factors in establishing an efficient handwriting style in early writing development?
- What might you need to address in terms of your own handwriting style to ensure that you are providing children with a good model?

Reflection for leader/manager

- What action do you need to take to ensure that there is a consistency of approach to letter formation across the practitioner team in your setting?

⇨

Consider in particular the use of exit and entry strokes in the handwriting that is provided as a model for children – on signs and labels around the setting; on handwritten messages that practitioners write with children and on the children's work.

- Consider the balance between the proportion of handwritten and computer-generated text used around the setting.
- How do you ensure that parents are fully aware of your approach to the model of handwritten script that you provide for the children? How might they be encouraged to support your approach?

One of the key questions here for early years practitioners is 'When should we embark on teaching letter formation?' One of the dilemmas involved in this decision is that at this point the practitioner must directly teach the skills involved. Letter formation is not something that children can discover for themselves through exploratory or imaginative play, and the 'formal' nature of teaching letter formation may cause some tension within a play-based curriculum. However, when the potential impact on handwriting fluency and efficiency of not intervening is considered, it is obvious that practitioners must carefully time and target their approach. Research has also suggested that poor handwriting development has a negative impact on composition in writing, since for writers struggling with handwriting, the amount of working memory needed to produce the script itself leaves little room for thinking about the message (Medwell and Wray, 2008) and it would seem obvious that a writer who finds handwriting a huge physical stress is unlikely to be enthusiastic about writing at length.

Sassoon (1990) suggests that as soon as children are able to write as much as their own names they should be taught how to form letters which 'move' correctly. As discussed earlier, the letters needed to write their own name are often the first that children will attempt, and since they then focus on writing their name repeatedly and for many different purposes, it is important for practitioners to ensure that those letters in particular are being formed correctly. Children who are encouraged to write 'emergently' will also commonly use the letters from their name in their messages, and so any 'bad habits' in the formation of these letters will be frequently reinforced in a setting that is rich in opportunities for writing and mark making. Many children are taught to write their names by a parent or carer and will often have used upper case letters. This word, in this form, will have taken on a special status as part of the child's expression of self and identity with home and family, and as such, any attempts to change it must be handled sensitively by practitioners.

In a setting that provides children with a wide range of mark-making opportunities, careful observation and analysis of samples of writing and mark making should enable the practitioner to identify a point at which children begin to use letter shapes or approximations of them. At this stage, children will not necessarily have begun to make a connection between the words that they intend to communicate in their message and the letter shapes they use; their phonological awareness may not have developed to the point where they can segment out the phonemes in a word so that they can make a decision about what letter to use to represent it. However, if they have begun to reproduce the letter shapes that are visually familiar to them in their writing, it is important that practitioners are confident that they are forming those letters correctly. This is an individualized approach to handwriting development, since not all children will be producing letters at the same stage; they may all use different letters in their emergent writing, and those children who do use letters will not necessarily form them incorrectly or need further support. In the early stages of writing development, it is certainly not necessary for practitioners to deliver letter formation practice activities to whole classes or even as an adult-led activity that every child is asked to participate in.

The current approach to phonics teaching recommended by the DCSF (2007) suggests that the starting point should be a range of activities to develop phonological awareness, the ability to distinguish individual phonemes (see Chapter 3). The key skill here in terms of writing is that of 'segmenting' – the ability to segment out the individual phonemes in a word so that the writer can make decisions about which letters are needed to spell it. Once this skill is established, children are ready to begin to learn the GPCs – learning which letters can be used to represent the sounds. At this point, it would also be useful to ensure that children are able to form the letters appropriately, since the intention is that they will begin to use their phonic knowledge in their writing. Regular, short handwriting activities which focus on the letter formation of the letter shapes being focused on in phonic work should ensure that children achieve an efficient style, which they can then continue to develop through extensive and various writing opportunities.

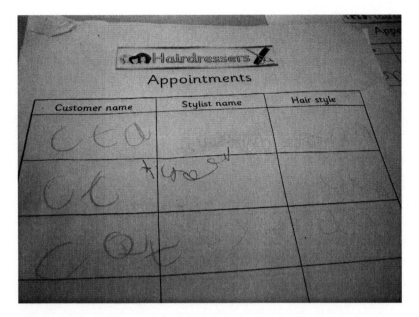

Photograph 6.3 A piece of child's writing (Photograph by L Nahmd-Williams)

Other approaches to presentation

In a discussion about handwriting, we should not actually confine ourselves to the presentation of handwritten script produced by the writer using a pen or pencil. Although the EYFS and the Early Learning Goal for handwriting (DCSF, 2008b) do not refer to other presentation skills the National Strategy Primary Framework for literacy (DCSF, 2009) adds objectives for effective use of a keyboard from Year 1 onwards. For example, in Year 1 children should learn to '. . . type their name and simple texts' (DCSF, 2009: Primary Framework for literacy: Learning objectives). If 'handwriting' in the EYFS was presented in the physical development area of learning and development then perhaps we could be justified in keeping the focus narrowly on the child's ability to 'Use a pencil and hold it effectively to form recognizable letters, most of which are correctly formed.' (DCSF, 2008b: 62), but since it obviously belongs in the communication, language and literacy area of learning and development, we must also consider the development of other presentation skills, particularly in the context of a society driven by digital forms of communication (Carrington, 2005; Waller, 2008). As we saw in Chapter 5 with the case study example of 'Jack' even children in the nursery are engaging with communication technologies, sending e-mails and text messages, using different methods of producing text. New methods of producing, using and sharing text are constantly being introduced to children's different social contexts. For example, I make and keep notes and lists for a wide range of purposes on my handheld mobile device using the touch screen keyboard to write. I also use this device to write text messages and e-mails and to surf the internet. The touch screen qwerty keyboard on this device is very small, 6 × 4 cm, and I 'type' on it using my right thumb only while the fingers of my right hand balance the device. Many mobile phones use the number keypad to input text and the use of one thumb to do this is common. I derive a similar pleasure from using this kind of device as I do from handwriting on good paper with a good fountain pen because I like using quality tools that meet my purposes well and I enjoy the sense of achievement in having developed a level of skill in using them.

The key issues here remain the same however; the writer must be able to produce typewritten script with speed and fluency in order that the message is communicated efficiently and so that the writer can devote the maximum level of concentration to composition. Each of these methods of presenting text has its own particular skill set, which involves some kind of physical, fine motor movement which in turn is supported by the gross motor skills needed to maintain posture and balance. They each have the potential for causing the writer physical pain if posture and position are not considered, and they are each judged by fluency, accuracy and speed. If these three elements are not sufficiently well developed, then information may be lost or forgotten before the writer is able to record it and the message may not be communicated clearly.

Conclusion

This chapter has explored what 'handwriting' might mean for children from birth to the age of 5 years. As a largely physical skill, which relies heavily on the successful development of both gross and fine motor movements, it may have seemed strange for it to be included as an aspect of the communication, language and literacy area of learning and development, but as we have seen, if children are not supported in developing their own fluent, comfortable and efficient handwriting style as part of their whole writing development, their ability to communicate successfully as writers will be affected.

Handwriting is not an aspect of learning and development that can be left to practitioners and teachers to 'pick up' in KS1 when children are deemed 'ready' or as part of a more formal, compartmentalized curriculum; the development of handwriting begins with the child's first movements and should be carefully considered as part of the holistic early years curriculum.

References

Carrington, V. (2005) 'New textual landscapes, information and early literacy', in Marsh, J. (ed.) *Popular Culture, New Media and Digital Literacy in Early Childhood*. London: Routledge, pp. 13–27

Cooper, L. and Doherty, J. (2010) *Physical Development*. London: Continuum.

DCSF (2007) *Letters and Sounds: Principles and Practice of High Quality Phonics*. London: DCSF

DCSF (2008a) *Mark Making Matters: Young Children Making Meaning in All Areas of Learning and Development*. London: DCSF

DCSF (2008b) *Setting the Standards for Learning, Development and Care for Children from Birth to Five; Practice Guidance for the Early Years Foundation Stage*. London: DCSF

DCSF (2009) 'Primary framework for literacy: Learning objectives', in *The National Strategies*. Available from: http://nationalstrategies.standards.dcsf.gov.uk/node/110237 [Accessed 20 October 2009]

Doherty, J. and Bailey, R. (2003) *Supporting Development and Physical Education in the Early Years*. Buckingham: Open University Press

Kress, G. (1997) *Before Writing: Rethinking the Paths to Literacy*. London: Routledge.

Medwell, J. and Wray, D. (2008) 'Handwriting – A forgotten language skill?'. *Language and Education*, 22, (1), 34–47

Rich, D. (2002) *More Than Words: Children Developing Communication, Language and Literacy*. London: The British Association for Early Childhood Education

Sassoon, R. (1990) *Handwriting: A New Perspective*. Cheltenham: Stanley Thornes

Siraj-Blatchford, I., Sylva, K., Muttock, S., Gilden, R. and Bell, D. (2002) *Researching Effective Pedagogy in the Early Years*. London: DfES

Waller, T. (2008) 'ICT and literacy', in Marsh, J. and Hallet, E. (eds) *Desirable Literacies: Approaches to Language and Literacy in the Early Years* (2nd edn). London: Sage, pp. 183–204

Conclusion

The series editors and authors hope that you find this book of interest and use to you in your professional work. If you would like to read more about the subject area, we recommend the following reading and websites to you.

Further reading

Alexander, R. (2004) *Towards Dialogic Teaching: Rethinking Classroom Talk.* York: Dialogos

Armstrong, M. (2006) *Children Writing Stories.* Berkshire: Open University Press

Beard, R. (ed) (1995) *Rhyme, Reading and Writing.* London: Hodder and Stoughton

Brock, A. and Rankin, C. (2008) *Communication Language and Literacy from Birth to Five.* London: Sage

Bromley, H. (2006) *Making My Own Mark – Play and Writing.* London: The British Association for Early Childhood Education

Browne, A. (2007) *Teaching and Learning Communication, Language and Literacy.* London: Paul Chapman

Browne, A. (2009) *Developing Language and Literacy 3–8* (3rd edn). London: Sage

Bruce, T. and Spratt, J. (2008) *Essentials of Literacy from 0–7.* London: Sage

Budgell, G. and Ruttle, K. (2008) *Penpals for Handwriting Foundation 1: Mark-Making and Creativity Teachers' Book* (2nd edn). Cambridge: Cambridge University Press

Cremin, T. and Dombey, H. (eds) (2007) *Handbook of Primary English in Initial Teacher Training.* Cambridge: UKLA/NATE

Crystal, D. (1995) *The Cambridge Encyclopedia of the English Language.* Cambridge: Cambridge University Press

Graddol, D., Cheshire, J. and Swann, J. (1994) *Describing Language.* Buckingham: Open University Press

Grainger, T. (1997) *Traditional Storytelling in the Primary Classroom.* Leamington Spa: Scholastic

Hall, N. and Robinson, A. (2003) *Exploring Writing and Play in the Early Years* (2nd edn). London: David Fulton

James, F. (1996) *Phonological Awareness.* Royston: UKLA

Johnston, J. and Nahmad-Williams, L. (2009) *Early Childhood Studies.* Harlow: Pearson Education

Johnston, R. and Watson, J. (2007) *Teaching Synthetic Phonics.* Exeter: Learning Matters

Lewis, D. (2001) *Reading Contemporary Picture Books: Picturing Text.* London: Routledge Falmer

Lindon, J. (2005) *Understanding Child Development.* London: Hodder Arnold

Norman, K. (ed.) (1992) *Thinking Voices: The Work of the National Oracy Project.* London: Hodder and Stoughton

Rich, D. (2002) *More Than Words: Children Developing Communication, Language and Literacy.* London: The British Association for Early Childhood Education

Sassoon, R. (2003) *Handwriting: The Way to Teach It* (2nd edn). London: Paul Chapman

Wells, G. (1986) *The Meaning Makers*. London: Hodder and Stoughton.

Whitehead, M. R. (2004) *Language and Literacy in the Early Years* (3rd edn). London: Sage

Wyse, D. (2007) *How to Help Your Child Read and Write*. London: Pearson Education

Useful websites

http://www.ican.org.uk/

http://www.speechteach.co.uk/p_resource/parent/devel_milestones.htm

http://www.afasic.org.uk/

http://www.literacytrust.org.uk/Database/earlyyears.html

http://www.st-andrews.ac.uk/soundanth/work/trevarthen/

http://www.rcslt.org/aboutslts/

http://www.teachingexpertise.com/articles/fostering-young-childrens-thinking-skills-3193

http://www.teachernet.gov.uk/teachingandlearning/EYFS/themes_principles/learning_development/
    creativity/

http://nationalstrategies.standards.dcsf.gov.uk/node/132707

http://www.btbetterworld.com

http://www.thecommunicationtrust.org.uk

http://www.talkingpoint.org.uk

http://www.standards.dcsf.gov.uk/phonics/

http://www.gtce.org.uk/teachers/rft/phonics0707/

http://nationalstrategies.standards.dcsf.gov.uk/eyfs/taxonomy/33692/33660/0/46384

http://www.standards.dfes.gov.uk/phonics/report.pdf

http://www.early-education.org.uk

http://www.literacytrust.org.uk

http://www.nha-handwriting.org.uk

If you would like to read more about other key areas of the EYFS, please see the following:

Creative Development, by Compton, A., Johnston, J., Nahmad-Williams, L. and Taylor, K. (London: Continuum, 2010)

Knowledge and Understanding of the World, by Cooper, L., Johnston, J., Rotchell, E. and Woolley, R. (London: Continuum, 2010)

Personal, Social and Emotional Development, by Broadhead, P., Johnston, J., Tobbell, C. and Woolley, R. (London: Continuum, 2010)

Physical Development, by Cooper, L. and Doherty, J. (London: Continuum, 2010)

Problem Solving, Reasoning and Numeracy, by Beckley, P., Compton, A., Johnston, J. and Marland, H. (London: Continuum, 2010)

Index